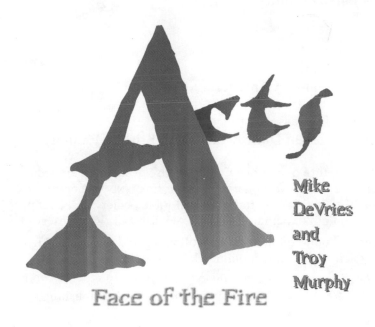

Acts

Mike
DeVries
and
Troy
Murphy

Face of the Fire

"No Limits" Discipleship Series

Barefoot Ministries
Kansas City, Missouri

ISBN 083-415-0069

Printed in the
United States of America

Editor: Bo Cassell
Cover Design: Doug Bennett and Kristina Phillips

Library of Congress Cataloging-in-Publication Data

DeVries, Mike.
   Acts : face of the fire / Mike DeVries and Troy Murphy.
   p. cm. — (No limits discipleship series ; bk. 2)
Summary: A devotional based on the book of Acts which provides, for each day, a reading, commentary on the passage, and suggested ways of incorporating the message into one's daily life.
   ISBN 0-8341-5006-9 (pbk.)
   1. Bible. N.T. Acts—Devotional literature. 2. Christian youth—Prayer-books and devotions—English. [1. Bible. N.T. Acts. 2. Holy Spirit. 3. Prayer books and devotions. 4. Christian life.] I. Murphy, Troy. II. Title. III. Series.

   BS2625.54.D48 2003
   226.6'0071—dc22

                              2003023581

Contents

Acknowledgments and Dedication

To my lifelong friend Jon Irving, You have walked with me, my friend, through much that life has thrown my way. You have been and always will be a faithful companion, a helper, my encourager. He is changing us. I can see His face in you. —Mike

To my lifelong friend Tom Marchant, who has literally faced many fires as a firefighter but has also seen the real *face in the fire* and has dedicated his life to helping others see His face as well. —Troy

With appreciation to the many people who were so important in the writing of this book:

To our families, who have given so much to make this project a reality—late nights, missed meals, and the "Where's Daddy?" "Oh, he's in the office typing."

To Tricia and Jamie—once again we are reminded of all that you are. You both are a gift of grace from God—a gift not deserved. We are blessed men.

To our church family at South County United—our greatest desire is that we would be saturated in the Holy Spirit as a church. Thank you for allowing us to be a part of the journey with you.

To Jeff Edmondson and Kevin Brown—Words cannot express our thanks for allowing us the creative freedom to dream. Partnering with you has been one of life's sweet joys.

To our God, our sustainer, our Creator—You are everything we have ever needed and ever will. Our lives are Yours.

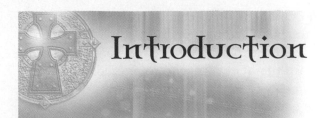

Introduction

Their Story, Our Story

Remember the followers of God in the desert of Sinai. They were pursuing a God who called them to be a nation, a people. He had forged an identity in them, calling them His own. They were no longer slaves under the rule of the Egyptians—they were now free. They were free *from* an identity, slavery, yet were freed *to* a new one, being the chosen people of God.

Let's fast forward. It's early in the first century, and the most amazing events have been happening. Long after the days of the desert, there appears the long-awaited one—the Messiah, *Jeshua*. Born in Bethlehem to a carpenter and a virgin, He owns nothing during His lifetime. He travels no more than 200 miles from His hometown. He has no formal education, no credentials.

He gathers a group of *talmidim* (followers). He walks the countryside and the city streets saying and doing the most amazing things. He heals. He raises the dead.

At the age of 33, this rabbi, Jesus, is crucified on a Roman cross one Friday. He is buried in a borrowed sepulchre. Yet at first light on Sunday, something happens that would change everything for the rest of time—He rises from the dead. He appears to His followers. He appears to many in the city and in the surrounding area. He ascends to heaven, leaving His followers to wait, holding onto His words "Stay in the city until you have been clothed with power from on high" (Luke 24:49).

This is a great climactic chapter in a great story. But the story is not finished. The next chapter is what happened after Jesus left the earth for heaven, and sent the Holy Spirit to be with the believers who remained. The Book of Acts is often considered to be the record of the actions of those early disciples.

However, the Book of Acts is ultimately not a story of the acts of the disciples but of the acts and the activity of the Holy Spirit. Acts is the story of the Spirit of God at work in the early followers of "the Way," who followed the teachings of Jesus. They were followers who were in passionate pursuit of God, living in a new reality, awakened to the power and person of the Holy Spirit.

The Hebraic mind-set saw the Scriptures as early chapters in a larger story. The Scriptures were *their* story, as much as it was the story of their ancestors. It was a living story. They saw themselves as connected to Moses crossing the Red Sea, and connected to every account of the people of God.

So it is with us today.

Acts is another chapter in the continuing epic story of God. It's the story of a people long ago, but it's also our story. This epic story is still being written today—in our hearts and lives.

Entering In #1

Betrothal

The story of the Scriptures is the story of pursuit. It's the story of the Creator God in pursuit of humanity as a lover pursues a beloved. God is in pursuit of you. You are His beloved, and He is your lover—the one who loves you with an unending love.

Now we don't always feel too comfortable with this kind of view. We like to keep God at a safe arm's length from us and our lives. We like to keep God in a box. We compartmentalize Him and divide Him with nice neat labels like "the God of the Old Testament" and "the God of the New."

The problem is that there's no such thing.

God is God. He's the God we see in the pages of the Old Testament and the same God we see in the New. He is a grace-filled, wrathful God. He is a holy and righteous, forgiving God. He is a fearful and awesome lover. He is the same yesterday, today, and forever (see Psalm 102:25-27; Hebrews 1:10-12; 13:8). He never changes. He doesn't have one plan and goal in the Old Testament and another in the New. His pursuit has always been and will always be the same—to be a lover connected to His beloved.

Betrothal is a concept that's lost on the modern reader but is filled with incredible imagery for the Middle Eastern reader. It was the custom of engagement in the Middle Eastern culture. It required the groom-to-be to visit the bride-to-be's father. At the meeting the two would discuss the "bride price," the amount the young man would have to pay the father for the privilege of marrying his daughter. Once the amount was agreed upon, the father would pour a glass of wine and hand it to the young man. The young man would in turn offer it to his intended bride and say, "This cup I offer you." If she agreed to the marriage proposal, she would drink from the glass.

> **Then he took the cup, gave thanks and offered it to them, and they all drank from it.**
> **"This is my blood of the covenant, which is poured out for many," he said to them.**
>
> —From Mark's account of the Last Supper
> (Mark 14:23-24)

The betrothed bride would then take a year to prepare herself for the wedding day. The betrothed groom would take the year to make preparations—financial plans, wedding plans, and home arrangements—all in hopes of coming back in a year ready for the celebration. He "went away" to prepare everything they would need for their new life together. Her responsibility during that time was to learn to be a wife, to respond to her lover as a beloved.

> **In my Father's house are many rooms; if it were not so, I would have told you. I am going there to prepare a place for you. And if I go and prepare a place for you, I will come back and take you to be with me that you also may be where I am.**
>
> —Jesus (John 14:2-3)

Get the picture yet? Jesus is saying, "You are My beloved, and I want to betroth you to Me in faithfulness." The story continues. Jesus was a bridegroom (John 3:27-29) coming to seek a bride. He was a lover seeking a beloved. We are that beloved. When we surrender ourselves to God, we are entering into a betrothal, a covenant with God.

Acts is the story of the betrothed bride of Christ living in covenant with God, and learning how to live in this new relationship. It's the story of the Holy Spirit, empowering and moving in the midst of His followers, and the response of His people to Him.

Luke, the physician and a follower of Jesus, penned the words to the Book of Acts. He wrote them as a chronicle of this amazing story of God's pursuit, hoping to share the story with Theophilus, a leading intellectual in the Roman middle class. His account is of the "acts of the Holy Spirit" moving in the midst of the Early Church.

As much as this is an ancient story, it is really our story as well. How will we respond to the Holy Spirit in our lives, in our world today? The same Holy Spirit you will read about in the book of Acts is active today. The same Holy Spirit at work in Peter and Paul and the others in that story is the same Holy Spirit working in you.

Day 1

You Are the Church

Encounter the Word

Read Acts 1:1-11.

Explore the Word

What's the first word you think of when you read the word "church"? Take a moment to write down on this page a list of words that come to mind.

Now be honest. How many of your words had to do with a building or location? How many of them were an emotion you have felt or currently feel about church?

All of us have an image of church. For some it may be a place of comfort. For others it may be the boring, un-connected, and irrelevant place "where God is." Nothing could be farther from the truth.

Reread Acts 1:6-8. Who is talking? What is He saying?

Jesus' disciples are asking Him about a physical place: "Lord, are you at this time going to restore the kingdom to Israel?" In other words, "Jesus are You going to change this place to be 'the kingdom of God'?" They wanted to see something spiritual manifested in the physical.

Jesus' answer is amazing: "You will receive power when the Holy Spirit comes on you; and you will be my witnesses in Jerusalem, and in all Judea and Samaria, and to the ends of the earth."

They wanted a place where the power of God would reside, in God's kingdom territory. Yet Jesus rejected that kind of thinking. "No, it's not about a place—it's about *you*. It's *in* you!" It's not a building or a location.

You are the Church. The essence of what the kingdom of God is lives in you if you're a follower of the Way. The Church is in you. As you gather with others, you're the Church. When you worship God, no matter where you are, you're the Church. The Church is people living in a new reality, empowered by the Holy Spirit, living in response to His leading.

Live the Word

Take a moment to meditate on (think deeply about) this reality. Quietly reflect on the word "Church." Allow your mind to be filled with images of the "Church." Start by visualizing various church buildings; begin to focus on faces of people.

Find a mirror, and look at yourself in it. As you look into your eyes, slowly say and reflect on the statement "I am the Church."

Spend a few moments in prayer, asking God to give you a new vision of the Church. Ask Him to burn into your heart the truth that people are the Church—moving, living, breathing, acting.

Day 2

Crying Out for God

Encounter the Word

Read Acts 1:12-26.

Explore the Word

We were moving from our old house to the house we live in now. My son Josh was all of six years old back then, and he wanted to help so badly. He picked up a box (one that *didn't* say "fragile") and headed out the door. When at last he reached the car, he lifted the box and tried to put it into the backseat. No luck. After a few hopeless attempts, he fell to the ground, trapped by the box on top of him.

"Want some help, Josh?"

"No thanks, Dad. I got it!"

We have a God who is ever present in our lives, yet we often feel that life is really all up to us. He asks us, "Want some help there?" and we reply, "No thanks, Dad. I got this one. I'll call you when I need you. See ya."

The disciples were in a situation that was bigger than they could ever solve. Yet instead of relying on their own intellect or their own judgment, they decided to seek God.

So what's it going to be? Seek God or get crushed by the box?

Live the Word

What are you facing today that seems insurmountable? Take a few minutes to write a letter to God, releasing your burden and asking Him for guidance and help. You'll be amazed at what He'll do if you allow Him.

Day 3

The Holy Spirit Enters

Encounter the Word

Read Acts 2:1-13.

Explore the Word

Think about a moment in your life when you anticipated something so much that you "just couldn't wait." Maybe it was a date on a calendar or a person you wanted to see—whatever it was, you "just couldn't wait."

The followers of Jesus had been waiting. In Luke 24:49 (recounted in Acts 1:3-5), Jesus was about to ascend to heaven and reminded His followers to stay in the city. He was going to send what the Father had promised: the Holy Spirit.

Stay in the city. Stay together. Watch. Wait. Something's going to happen.

The disciples obeyed. They waited. Fifty days passed from the first Sunday after Passover, when Jesus was crucified and buried and had risen from the dead, to the day of Pentecost. They waited. They watched. They anticipated. What would happen? When would it happen?

Then it came.

They were gathered together. The room filled with a sound like a violent wind. Fire flashed from heaven and came to rest on each person in the room.

And they began to speak. Each one spoke in a different language of the known world. And people came, each one hearing their native tongue spoken. What was going on? Who were these people? What were they talking about?

The Holy Spirit had come, and the world would never be the same again. The anticipation was over. He had come. There was a new and fresh wind blowing in the ancient cradle of religion.

The Holy Spirit had come to guide this new band of followers, to usher them into a new way of relating to God. This was the way promised long ago in Ezekiel 36:26-27, "I will give you a new heart and put a new spirit in you; I will remove from you your heart of stone and give you a heart of flesh. And I will put my Spirit in you and move you to follow my decrees and be careful to keep my laws."

The waiting was over. God's Holy Spirit had come.

Live the Word

Can you think of one area in which you've been waiting for God? Know this for sure: God sees and hears. In the meantime, grab a Bible concordance and look up all the times the word "wait" is used in the Book of Psalms. Take a moment to write down some truths that you can take away from the verses you find.

Day 4
The Holy Spirit Speaks

Encounter the Word

Read Acts 2:14-41.

Explore the Word

We're regularly bombarded with noise. Think about it. How much time do we take to be silent each day? Most families have more than one television set. I even know someone who has one in his bathroom. We have CD players in our homes and in our cars. We listen to music when we're using the computer. Mobile phones beep, ring, and sing to us—no matter where we are. Everywhere we turn, we're bombarded with noise.

But does it have to be that way?

I think we're addicted to noise not because we like it but because we're scared of silence. Noise is easy—it drowns out the voices and pressure and allows us to escape.

The truth of the matter is this: we're scared of the silence because it's in silence that we're confronted with the hollow condition of our souls. Rather than face the silence and be left alone with our thoughts, we numb our souls with noise.

God speaks in silence. He speaks to us when we slow down long enough to hear, when we unplug from the noise and truly listen to what He has for us.

In today's reading we find Peter addressing a large crowd. The crowd had gathered around the cluster of Christ followers, because they had seen the Spirit visibly at work in them. They were ready to listen.

"Brothers, what shall we do?" they exclaimed after having their ears opened and their hearts pierced by what Peter said. When the Holy Spirit speaks, He cuts through the noise and speaks directly to the soul. If you listen, you can't help but be changed.

God is speaking. Are you listening?

Live the Word

Take a half hour sometime today and be silent. Find a place in your house or somewhere close by where you can spend that time without talking to anyone or listening to anything. Spend the time being silent—thinking, praying, meditating. Ask God to fill your mind not with noise but with His thoughts and heart. It may take some time to clear your head so that you can hear Him. Write down what you hear from God no matter what it is. Take time to absorb silence into your life. Let it speak to you. Let it heal you. Let it relax and refresh you. Listen to your own breathing. "Be still and know that I am God" (Psalm 46:10).

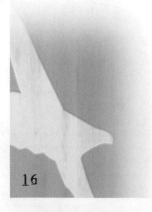

Day 5

Responding to the Holy Spirit

Encounter the Word

Read Acts 2:42-47.

Explore the Word

Listening is only half the spiritual conversation. With listening comes response. "Do not merely listen to the Word . . . Do what it says" (James 1:22).

If the Master of the universe speaks to you, you're left with one of two responses—to worship and obey, or to walk away and risk becoming hardened to His voice.

Notice the list of things that were going on in the lives of Christ's followers at the time. They were living in response to all that the Holy Spirit was doing in their lives. People were listening to the message and teachings of Jesus and were changed! Not just in their thinking, not just in their beliefs, not just in their attitudes—these followers of "the Way" were changed to the core. They lived differently because of the Holy Spirit.

Live the Word

How has your life changed since you decided to be a Christ follower? Take a few minutes to write down as many ways as you can think of. As you look over that list, celebrate what God has done in your life. Thank Him for each of those areas in which you've been changed. You might even want to start another list—a list of areas that you would still like to see changed. As a final way of celebrating all that God has done, call someone in your small group and share lists with each other. Pray and bless God for all He has done in your lives.

Entering In #2

Image

Contemplation

When my family and I moved to Mission Viejo, California, my wife and I were looking for a house with a nice backyard. Each of us wanted a backyard for very different reasons. My wife wanted a place for the kids to play. I wanted a place where I could put up a hammock and pass out. Both of us could agree on one thing: we wanted to have a backyard that we could grow something in.

My goal was to plant an orange tree, so I did what any man would do—I went to the Internet to find out about having an orange tree, and within minutes I was printing out a picture of what my future orange tree would look like. With image in hand, I did the next thing any man would do—I went to Home Depot.

I figured all I needed was all the right stuff, and I would "build" an orange tree. Oak barrel, dirt, a stick (I mean a trunk), leaves, oranges, and a load of duct tape.

So now I have an orange tree. Only the oranges don't taste too good.

Images are the substance without the reality. Ever notice that we can look the part, have all the right ingredients, yet be no closer to the reality? We try to say the right things and do the right things, thinking that if we construct something that looks like that image, we can somehow attain the reality of the image. Yet all we're left with is a hollow and cheap imitation of the real thing.

You can do all the right "things"—read your Bible, go on mission trips, share the message of Jesus with your friends—you can have whatever "spiritual ingredients" you think you may need but still be no closer to the real thing than my orange tree. My orange tree had all the right ingredients, but it was missing the reality—life itself.

True spiritual transformation happens from the inside out, not the outside in.

Reread Acts 2:42-47. If we're not careful, we can easily fall into the trap of making Acts 2:42-47 into a roadmap, or an "image," of what it means to be a Christ follower. We read what other believers did and we try to do the same things—forgetting that they did these things outwardly because the Spirit had already changed them inwardly. Being a Christ follower is so much more than conforming to a checklist—it's an inner reality. The reality of Acts 2:42-47 shows what living in response to the Holy Spirit looks like.

Communication

As a small group, when you get together, talk about the metaphor of the orange tree. What did you learn from it? How is your life like the orange tree? What practical steps will you take to move to a position of responding to the Holy Spirit from an inner love rather than an outer religiousness?

Community

As a group, do a study on what the role of the Holy Spirit is in the life of the Christ follower. What does it mean to "live by the Spirit"? Dig into the Scriptures to find your answers. Have a few study resources on hand at your group, such as extra Bibles, a concordance, a Bible dictionary or Bible encyclopedia, and a commentary on the New Testament.

Day 1

Ministry Along the Way

Encounter the Word

Read Acts 3:1-10.

Explore the Word

Have you ever encountered people who were begging for food or money? How did it make you feel? During the days of this story from Acts, the Jews observed prayer at the Temple three times a day. One Temple entrance that was very popular among the people was the "Beautiful Gate." At this entrance beggars and crippled people would line the walkway to beg for money. It was also a popular entrance for the religious leaders of the time, and many of them were looking for a way to show just how religious they were.

Many of these leaders would give money to the needy people. This was considered a very praiseworthy act of a good religious leader, and it was an everyday practice. Now, it is a good thing to help the poor, but these religious leaders did it in ways that would draw attention to themselves. Someone watching might get the feeling that they cared more about the show of religion—appearing generous—than they cared about actually helping the poor.

Now imagine thousands of people coming in through this gateway and hundreds and hundreds of sick, blind, crippled and poor people shouting for money, mercy, anything they could get. Now imagine Peter and John in the flow of this crowd moving quickly toward the Temple for prayer. Now picture them stopping as they hear this one beggar's voice. People were bumping and moving around, and Peter put his eyes right on this man whose unusable legs were folded underneath him. Then Peter said, "Silver or gold I do not have, but what I have I give you. In the name of Jesus Christ of Nazareth, walk." What do you think this beggar thought of that statement? Maybe he was disappointed at first, but I guarantee that when he heard the command "Walk," and felt the strength return to his legs, he felt the hairs on his body stand up with excitement. He was healed!

Live the Word

Peter and John had already seen God's Holy Spirit do some amazing things to grow the church, but at this moment they were living out their routine. They were just going to pray. They always did that. Here they were on the *steps* of the Temple, the most Holy Place of their known history, and the Holy Spirit chose to start a spiritual fire *outside* that place. You see, the Holy Spirit is not defined by or simply a resident of a building—He lives inside people, the new temple. You're a walking temple that can be used at any moment.

What are the steps you travel every day of your life? School, work, home, the store, the mall? Wherever those steps may be, be careful to be listening to His voice and not miss the ministry along the way. There are people who need Jesus—not you, not your advice, not even your money, but the power of Jesus in you. Have you ever heard the Holy Spirit's voice and prayed with someone you didn't know? Or helped someone who never asked? Or shared Jesus with someone you just met? Take some time today to read Paul's challenge in Colossians 4:2-6, and pray that God will open a door for you to serve Him along the way.

Day 2

Working in Jesus' Name

Encounter the Word

Read Acts 3:11-26.

Explore the Word

The religious leaders of the time were walking by the gate called Beautiful to gain glory and religious popularity. The beggars and crippled people were at the gate to gather some financial gain. God, however, requires that we not gain for ourselves but rather *lose* ourselves. In the midst of the miraculous, Peter made it very clear: "It's not about me." He healed "in the name of Jesus Christ of Nazareth," giving full credit to Him. At this point Peter had the chance to become a popular religious leader, a healer! But Peter not only clarified that it was Jesus who had done the healing—he went on to tell the people how far off they were from being holy, that in fact they were guilty of a crime—that of killing Jesus, who gave the power and authority to heal.

Live the Word

Part of the sinful nature is to seek honor for oneself, to work in one's own name. Who gets the credit for your life, for all the things you do, for all that you're becoming?

What are practical ways you can begin to give credit to God for the Holy Spirit's work in you? Get out a journal or piece of paper and write a response that you could use when people try to give you credit. It doesn't need to be long or theological but simply your expression of "in His name." Reread Colossians 4:2-6, and ask the Holy Spirit for boldness to respond when called on.

Day 3

The Holy Spirit Gives Boldness

Encounter the Word

Read Acts 4:1-22.

Explore the Word

Several weeks before the scene in this passage, Peter had denied Jesus three times. Yet in this scene we see some other power in Peter. He was not himself.

The Beautiful gate led into Court of the Gentiles, where any non-Jew could enter the Temple and where money changers exchanged foreign money for Temple currency. Through this court and onto the scene came a group of religious leaders called the Sadducees, who were the wealthy aristocrats of that time, influential in the religious and political system. They heard that someone had healed a cripple. The high priest's right-hand man, the captain, showed up. This event would have created much attention, and he most likely would have brought the Temple police with him. Hundreds, probably thousands of people looked at Peter and John as they said, "Not us but Jesus!" The crowd starts believing. They had not seen or heard of anything like this since the Carpenter from Nazareth had died. Saying that the crucified Jesus had healed this man did not sit well with the Sadducees, whose belief system did not allow for the possibility of anyone rising from the dead. They were also concerned with any disorder that might disrupt their good political standing. They arrested Peter and John, and decided to sleep on the decision of what to do with them.

The next day the Holy Spirit spoke through Peter.

> **When they saw the courage of Peter and John and realized that they were unschooled, ordinary men, they were astonished and they took note that these men had been with Jesus (Acts 4:13).**

The Holy Spirit had given boldness to a disloyal, cowardly, uneducated, fisherman. The crowd noticed his courage and made the association—these men were followers of Jesus.

Live the Word

Have you ever stopped to think about the concept that maybe God wants you right in the middle of adversity? Right where no one could ever say you got through it by yourself. The Holy Spirit loves those places. They're where He has the opportunity, if we allow Him, to give a boldness and authority that cannot be explained.

James 1:2-4 says, "Consider it pure joy, my brothers, whenever you face trials of many kinds, because you know that the testing of your faith develops perseverance. Perseverance must finish its work so that you may be mature and complete, not lacking anything."

Maybe God and the Holy Spirit are up to something in your life. They might be building your character, your faith, your endurance, or your maturity. Boldness in adversity comes only from the Holy Spirit, and when we allow Him to work, we have an authority that's spiritually powerful and changes lives. Take a walk and reflect on the trials you've gone through and look back at how they were handled. Also think about any trial you might presently be experiencing, and ask God to help you surrender to the Holy Spirit's power. Ask Him to grow you up through this experience.

Day 4

Exalt the Father

Encounter the Word

Read Acts 4:23-31.

Explore the Word

After Peter and John defended the authority and power to heal given to them in Jesus' name, they headed right for their own church community. They shared their story, and all their fellow believers were united and prayed (v. 24). I love how *The Message* translates it: "Hearing the report, they lifted their voices in a wonderful harmony in prayer." What broke out was not an award ceremony or self glorified speeches, but a wonderful concert of prayer. In verses 24-30 we get to see this prayer, which gave honor to God for being at work in the past as well as in their present moment.

Live the Word

In today's verses we get a picture of a radically changed group of Jesus followers. They are confident and focused on a cause that has their life's full attention—to exalt God. "Exalt" simply means "to lift up." When Peter and John shared with their community, there is no self focused "touchdown dance"—their first reflex was to "exalt" God in prayer and worship.

Who is your community? Who do you gather and celebrate with? What Holy Spirit activity in your life do you have to share with your community? If these are difficult questions for you to answer, then take some time to ask God where your community is and how you can begin to exalt God together with them.

Day 5
The Holy Spirit Creates Unity

Encounter the Word

Read Acts 4:32-37.

Explore the Word

In today's reading we see the Holy Spirit transforming people so much that they were selling homes and property and throwing the money at the apostles' feet! (Apostle means "sent one" and was often used to designate the original 12 disciples, or anyone sent out with special authority.) They offered these voluntary acts of love to meet the needs of others. They felt responsible for each other. The Holy Spirit is unifying the hearts and minds of these followers to love God with all their hearts but also to love each other.

Live the Word

Have you ever experienced a great sense of unity in your community (your church)—a unity of love or of purpose—a unity that cares for any need around it no matter what it costs? Why don't we experience this as much today? Is it because we are selfish, materialistic, or just not transforming? Take some time to list all the "stuff" you have. Now ask the Holy Spirit to put into your heart and mind a need that's around you. It could be a friend, a family member, a neighbor—any need you've been made aware of. Now sell something. That's right—sell one or more of those things on your list, and give the money to the one who needs it. Then encourage a friend to voluntarily love someone else.

Entering In #3

Reaction

Contemplation

Plans. We make them for everything today. We make wedding plans, plans for the weekend, plans to graduate, plans for exercise, plans for a date—plans for everything. Many of us even have a plan for our spiritual lives. Don't misunderstand me—plans are not bad themselves; it's just that our spiritual lives are not really ours to plan. You see, the Holy Spirit is in charge of creating change within us and (eventually) a spiritual reaction.

The word "reaction" simply means a response to something else. We've watched the journey of the Holy Spirit as He has inhabited the lives of these disciples and their followers. Their reaction has been unplanned and powerful. For example, look at Acts 2:42-47. Do you see any verses that would lead you to believe that they planned this revival? Was their plan to have a church garage sale to raise money for the poor? Do you find a plan for having a "miraculous signs" service? Get the point? Look at Acts 3:1-10. Do you find that Peter and John were planning to do some healing that day? Look at Acts 4:32-35. Do you find a "home selling" campaign plan being unfolded? The Book of Acts cannot be read as a strategic plan to produce ministry in people's lives but as an account of people who are so in love with Jesus and filled with the Holy Spirit that they have a natural spiritual reaction. Instead of trying to "look" spiritual and trying to "do" spiritual things, we might be better off opening ourselves up to the love of God and allowing the Spirit freedom to work in us.

Communication

Look at the following two verses:

- In his *heart* a man *plans* his course, but the LORD determines his steps (Proverbs 16:9).
- Many are the *plans* in a man's *heart*, but it is the Lord's purpose that prevails (Proverbs 19:21).

Two key words to observe are "plans" and "heart." God allows and even wants us to plan, but it's something that starts in our hearts and is then handed over to whatever God's purpose is. We cannot plan the work of God in ourselves or others. We can hand our lives over to God and let Him create in us a reaction to the new life the Holy Spirit creates in us.

Community

This is a difficult concept to try and put into our lives. The very act of planning can seem contrary to what we've just discussed, but here's a suggested starting point: prayer. If you want to see a community of believers begin to have a spiritual reaction, then pray together. Pray as often as you possibly can. Pray that God will change your hearts so that your lives will become a reaction of love for God.

Day 1

The Holy Spirit Purifies

Encounter the Word

Read Acts 5:1-11.

Explore the Word

Contrary to what some may believe, early Christ follow-ers did not sell everything they had and live a commu-nal lifestyle. They did see their personal property as be-longing to God and free to be used for meeting the needs in their community. Sometimes followers would sell something and bring it to meet the needs of the Body of Christ.

Barnabas did such a thing in Acts 4:36-37. It was a spon-taneous act of giving prompted by the Holy Spirit. He didn't have to, but he did it as a response of gratitude to God.

Ananias and Sapphira, on the other hand, were another matter. They sold a plot of land voluntarily but kept back a portion of it for themselves, giving the rest under the appearance that it was the entire amount. They didn't have to give all the money—that was not a requirement—so why the deception? Apparently they wanted to have the appearance that they were something they weren't. They wanted to appear more religious, more spiritual than they really were—to look the same as Barnabas without having the heart of Barnabas.

God dealt directly with them to make a point: "I don't want your religious appearance. I want your heart. I want your acts of mercy and compassion to flow as a re-sponse from your heart."

Live the Word

Why do you do the religious things that you do? Select someone from your small group in whom you can confide. Ask him or her to hold you accountable for the "religious" things you do. Be honest with him or her about your motivation for why you do what you do. Allow this person to ask you tough questions about your so-called "spiritual" habits.

Day 2

Respect for the Holy Spirit

Encounter the Word

Read Acts 5:12-16.

Explore the Word

Today's reading says something amazing. Did you catch it? "No one dared to join them [the believers], even though they were highly regarded by the people" (Acts 5:13).

The Holy Spirit was doing so many amazing things in the midst of the believers that people were afraid of joining their meeting at Solomon's Colonnade, even though many were being "added to their number" (v. 14). The text even states that the believers were held in high regard by the people.

How different it is today! Talk to various people you may encounter during the day, and ask them this question: "What do you think about when you hear the word 'Christians'?" The vast majority will not utter the words "high regard." More often than not, words like "intolerant," "narrow-minded," "backward," or "judgmental" will be what you hear. Sad, isn't it?

Most of the "nonfollowers" that I have been around have those types of opinions. They've been burned by religious people—where their only encounter has been a negative act of judgmental, holier-than-thou self-righteousness.

What would nonfollowers think of our churches today? Would they be scared to join our church meeting because we were so like Christ that we were doing the same things He did? Would they be scared to join us because our fellowship with the Spirit was so dynamic that those in the midst who brought deception and corruption were instantly struck dead? Or would they be scared to join because they were afraid of being rejected—judged unworthy by an unloving group who called all outsiders to live up to their standard before they would accept them?

Live the Word

Find a quiet place where you will not be disturbed for at least a half hour. Read John 4:1-42, and consider the following questions.

- How did Jesus deal with the woman at the well? What did He say and do?

- What was the result of His exchange with the woman at the well?

- What was Jesus' point in His teaching with the disciples (vv. 32, 34-38)?

- What can you learn from Jesus and His teachings?

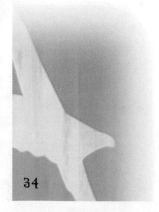

Day 3

Christian Counterculture

Encounter the Word

Read Acts 5:17-42.

Explore the Word

Why is it that we don't tell the truth? Why don't we say "Being a follower of Jesus is a decision we make to enter a countercultural movement, one that will cost us. Your life may not be easier; in fact, it will be filled with more difficult decisions than you ever faced before choosing to be a Christ follower."

We're not called to live culturally compatible lives. Our faith places us in direct opposition to our world. As a follower of Jesus, you're part of a countercultural movement of the Holy Spirit, just as Peter and the apostles were. They counted the cost of what it meant to be a follower of Jesus, and so should we. They were flogged and warned, but "they never stopped teaching and proclaiming the good news that Jesus is the Christ" (5:42). For them, no cost could compare to the incredible reality they knew in the Holy Spirit.

Live the Word

Look up the word "counterculture" or "countercultural" in the dictionary, and write down what you find there. Take a few minutes and write down what that means for you and your life. How is your life countercultural right now? In what areas of your life is Jesus calling you to live more countercultural? What will you do about those areas?

Day 4

Full of the Holy Spirit: Part 1

Encounter the Word

Read Acts 6:1-7.

Explore the Word

Because of the rapid growth of the Early Church, there were more things to be done than pairs of hands to do them. Some were having their needs met, while others were still waiting. Something needed to be done. More people were needed to serve and lead. "Brothers, choose seven men from among you who are known to be full of the Spirit and wisdom" (Acts 6:3).

Our society would tell us to find a person who has experience. Find a person with charisma and influence. Find just the right person for the job. When the disciples were looking to fill the need, what were God's criteria? God was looking for someone full of the Spirit and wisdom.

God is not looking for people who have all the right abilities. He doesn't want someone with influence or power. Rather, He's looking for someone who's in touch with the Holy Spirit. Is that where you are today?

Live the Word

Consider the following questions:

- What would a life look like that's saturated and "full of the Spirit"?
- What keeps us from being saturated with the Holy Spirit?
- What areas of your life are not under the control of the Holy Spirit?
- What is God calling you to in those areas?

Day 5

Full of the Holy Spirit: Part 2

Encounter the Word

Read Acts 6:8-15.

Explore the Word

Yesterday we began our investigation into what it means to be "full of the Spirit." In today's reading we encounter Stephen, one of the seven selected to take care of the widows and make sure they were being fed.

To get a better understanding of what it means to be full of the Holy Spirit, read Galatians 5:16-26. In this text Paul describes what it means to "live by the Spirit." He also describes the "fruit of the Spirit," which is the supernatural result of being saturated with the Holy Spirit.

Read the Galatians passage through five times slowly. After each reading, make a few notes on five separate pieces of paper of what you see, one for each reading. Don't repeat ideas or points, but rather write down after each reading something fresh from the passage. You can elaborate on a point that you made before, but the purpose is to allow the text to saturate your heart and mind. This may take you up to an hour, but it will be well worth the time and energy.

Live the Word

After your five readings consider the following questions:

- What does it mean to live by the Spirit?

- What are some of the costs of living by the Spirit?

- Notice verse 25. We are encouraged to "keep in step with the Spirit." How do we do just that?

Entering In #4

Appearances

Contemplation

I was cleaning out my garage a few months back and came across a box. I peeled back the tape and opened it, wondering what kind of treasure I was going to find. The box was filled with trophies—baseball trophies, football trophies, and soccer trophies, all from years gone long ago.

Think about this: what do trophies really stand for? Trophies are something that communicates to others, "I did it!" They are external markers to those around us that we're something special, that we accomplished some feat, some goal.

I wonder how much of our spirituality is nothing more than a trophy, an external marker of our spiritual accomplishments, shined up on the outside, on display for others to marvel at.

Jesus dealt harshly with people who were "externally spiritual," whose religion was practiced as a sort of a trophy for others to see. He often collided with some of the leading religious leaders of His day, called Pharisees:

> "Woe to you, teachers of the law and Pharisees, you hypocrites! You clean the outside of the cup and dish, but inside they are full of greed and self-indulgence. Blind Pharisee! First clean the inside of the cup and dish, and then the outside also will be clean. Woe to

you, teachers of the law and Pharisees, you hypo-crites! You are like whitewashed tombs, which look beautiful on the outside but on the inside are full of dead men's bones and everything unclean. In the same way, on the outside you appear to people as righteous but on the inside you are full of hypocrisy and wickedness." (Matthew 23:25-28)

Amazing! He called the leading religious leaders of His day decorated graves, appearing bright and shiny, but full of death and decay. He said they were nothing but play actors, inwardly lawless. In other words, they were actually far from the law, the righteousness that God re-quired—ironically the very thing they were holding up as their trophy!

Back to our question—why do you do the spiritual activ-ities you do? Is it out of appearance's sake (like Ananias and Sapphira)? Is it out of duty? Where do our trophies belong? Back in the box they go.

Communication

Read Matt. 5:3-10 and allow the words to penetrate your heart. Read them through a couple of times—out loud, si-lently—very slowly letting each word sink deeply into your heart. Take out a piece of paper and rewrite these eight verses in your own words. Bring that piece of paper with you, along with a trophy, to your small-group meeting.

Community

In your small group have one person read Matt. 5:3-10 from the Scriptures. Allow everyone to read his or her rewritten version of it, share how the contemplation im-pacted him or her, and what some of his or her "spiritu-al trophies" are. After each person shares, pray as a group for that individual. Keep going until each person has had a turn.

Day 1

The Holy Spirit Gives Wisdom

Encounter the Word

Read Acts 7:1-53.

Explore the Word

The Synagogue of Freedmen (which was an ironic name for them) had seized Stephen and interrogated him. They tried to fabricate lies to convict him.

This provides opportunity for Stephen to speak to the high priests. He recounted the life of Abraham, Joseph, Moses, and David, which is the all-important blood line for the Messiah, Jesus. He also made his argument that all these men lived lives of radical obedience for whatever God asked of them and did not let the past or traditions become their gods. He then said to those present, "You always resist the Holy Spirit." Last, Stephen accused these men of disobedience and rebellion, which ultimately led to their greatest crime: murdering God's Son.

Live the Word

Do you ever think about how great it would be to defend your faith? Or rather, maybe it scares you because you don't feel you know enough to be able to do it. This story about Stephen is a great reminder to all of us that it's the Holy Spirit's job to defend the faith. No amount of education can do what the Holy Spirit can do. He gives wisdom, grace, power, and authority.

Take a walk and simply talk with the Holy Spirit. Identify areas of your life that you have not surrendered fully to Him. Give them up, and be transformed.

Day 2

Seeing Things Differently

Encounter the Word

Read Acts 7:54-8:1.

Explore the Word

Imagine this scene: Stephen finishes his speech, which basically accuses the top religious officials of the city of being murderers. Acting in a fury and an uncontrollable rage, this mob of respected religious leaders dragged Stephen out and stoned him—throwing rocks at him until he died. In all of this Stephen had a peace and a calm that can come only from God. The Holy Spirit had transformed Stephen completely.

Live the Word

How do you respond when unwarranted anger, fury, and rage are directed toward you? Do you use more anger and rage to counter the attack? Jesus taught that we're to be a people who do not return anger for anger but instead return love for anything and everything that comes our way. The reality is that apart from the Holy Spirit we cannot do it. We must give Him the reins and trust Him. When we can do that, we don't see the angry distorted faces of those who are throwing the rocks, but our eyes are on Jesus. When you come face-to-face with a friend who hurts you intentionally, or when you have a family member who unloads his or her rage on you, how will you respond?

Again, ask the Holy Spirit to transform your heart and mind to be able to respond with peace and love. In your mind come up with a phrase or thought that will help you in times like these to focus on Christ.

Day 3

The Holy Spirit Uses Everything

Encounter the Word

Read Acts 8:1-8.

Explore the Word

The new community of believers was on a spiritual high, thousands coming to Christ, and now this: Stephen's murder by the Jewish leaders. The believers were fearful for their lives as Saul and the Jewish leaders dragged Christ's followers out of their homes to beat and imprison them. The text says that the believers began to scatter, and yet notice this— they "preached the word wherever they went" (v. 4). As tragic as Stephen's death was, it caused the new believers to scatter and share this Good News! Just when it all looked like the end, the Holy Spirit used it for a new beginning. God's plan to let all nations know of His love and salvation was spread out like a blazing forest fire.

Live the Word

Forest fires are a destructive force, but did you know that they're a natural and important function in our world's ecosystem? Fires often clear the clutter from a forest floor which creates new space and ideal growing conditions for new life. So the death of something can mean new life for others. Sound familiar? Stephen's death was not an end but a beginning of a master plan that God had all along.

Romans 8:27-28 says, "He knows us far better than we know ourselves . . . and keeps us present before God. That's why we can be so sure that every detail in our lives of love for God is worked into something good." (TM). Get out your Bible, read these verses, and memorize them.

Day 4

The Holy Spirit Can't Be Bought

Encounter the Word

Read Acts 8:9-25.

Explore the Word

The "scattering stories" are unfolding, and we see that Philip has traveled down to Samaria and is preaching about Jesus. The Holy Spirit is doing amazing things through Philip, which catches the attention of one called Simon, a boastful sorcerer who practices forms of magic from healing to astrology, which compelled the people of that time to follow him. The text says that the people of Samaria believed that he was the divine "Great Power." Even though this power was being used to help people, it was not from God but from demons.

Meanwhile, the Holy Spirit is doing more amazing works through Philip, Peter, and John. In fact, the miracles done by the Holy Spirit amazed this magician Simon! Ultimately he believes. But what does he believe? A short while later we see that he offers to pay the disciples for the ability to give the power of the Holy Spirit to people at will. Simon is strongly confronted by Peter and accused of having an unclean heart. Simon repents and asks Peter to pray for him.

Live the Word

You can't buy it or earn it. God's gift is just that, His to give to whomever He desires. Simon fell prey to two of the oldest temptations in life: power and prestige. Simon had power and control over the people of his town, when along came a greater power. Now he was no longer the top village magician. No longer did people follow and honor him. He himself is so impressed with this new power, that he figures if you can't beat 'em, join 'em. So he starts following. He may have been somewhat sincere, but his desire to know the God behind the miracles is clouded by his greed to control and master the magic. If he no longer has the greatest power in town, then he will no longer be the greatest in the eyes of the people of the town. No more "Great Power." No more prestige. So he tries to buy them back. The only problem is, you can't buy God. You can't control the Holy Spirit. God does not *perform* for us at our every whim, answering prayers at the push of a button. If you can't buy or earn the power of the Holy Spirit, how do you get it? You receive it as a gift. You humble yourself and surrender your control to God's will.

So few fully receive Jesus the as Lord of their lives and allow the Holy Spirit full control. Can you be a Christian without letting the Holy Spirit take full control? Many debate this issue, but one thing is clear: The filling of the Holy Spirit is not up for purchase! The Spirit's power is not a trick that we can show off but a transforming gift from God that will change you from the inside out. What are you on the inside? Are you a "spiritual magician"? Ask God to purify your heart and get rid of any false spiritual action that does not come from a pure heart.

Day 5

The Holy Spirit Leading

Encounter the Word

Read Acts 8:26-50.

Explore the Word

In today's passage we see Philip leave a large ministry in Samaria for the desert. He heard and obeyed the Holy Spirit's leading to drop what he was doing and go meet one person, an Ethiopian. Philip arrived at his destination and was given more instructions to "stand next to the chariot."

Philip started up a conversation that eventually led to the man's knowing and believing in Jesus. Philip then baptized him. Philip left his ministry with many people to see one life changed.

Live the Word

Who could have known what the Holy Spirit was doing back then? Big ministry is not the only ministry the Holy Spirit uses. We get so caught up today in what is big and popular in our Christian circles that we miss the one life God wants us to "stand next to." Would you have left the big ministry for the small? Are you still and quiet enough to hear the leadings of the Holy Spirit?

Find a large park or area where there's nothing but God's creation, and take an hour or two just to listen to what the Holy Spirit is asking of you. If you hear Him, respond in that moment. Don't wait to figure it all out. Whether you hear something in that moment or not, make this a regular time in your week's schedule simply to listen to the Holy Spirit.

Entering In #5

Awakening

Contemplation

"Wake up!" The father was shouting at his drunken son who had passed out on the floor. "Wake up!" A girl nudges her friend to get her ready for a camp night raid. "Wake up!" A mother picks up her new born for her feeding. "Wake up!" A doctor stares at a patient after a critical surgery. "Wake up!" God is whispering to His children to let the Holy Spirit take control.

Waking up physically can be difficult, but waking up spiritually is a miracle of God. Nothing compares to experiencing a genuine awakening. The Book of Acts is an account of people awakening to the Holy Spirit's control over their lives. Awakenings are powerful. They're awesome, because you see in a person some reaction and character you never saw before. You might even say that they're not themselves—and you would be right! They're *not* themselves—they're the Holy Spirit's. This week's readings highlight several awakenings among God's people. Moving from the awakening of Stephen and his death under persecution, we now see the dramatic change of the *persecutor*—as the Holy Spirit lays hold of the life of Saul. Saul and Peter both will be awakened by God to find that He is bigger—and has bigger plans—than they have ever dreamed.

Communication

No one wants to loose control. It's a sign of weakness or not being responsible. Yet the New Testament scriptures encourage people to "let go!" When we let go, God takes control by His Holy Spirit, and our lives begin to look like Jesus. Zechariah 4:6 says, "'Not by might nor by power, but by my Spirit,' says the LORD Almighty." Our spiritual efforts mean nothing without the Spirit of God there to wake us up to Him.

What about you—are you awake? Has the Holy Spirit been given full reign of your life? Have you let go of the control in your life? Take some time to reread these verses, and ask the Holy Spirit to take control of your whole life. Ask Him to awaken you spiritually.

Community

To be awakened is like being shaken from a sleepy spiritual slumber. We wake up to take action. It's like an athlete who has found his or her game. It's like the student who has found his or her subject. We begin serving on all cylinders. When you surrender to God, it allows Him to fully access the gifts and talents He has given you. That's when your service starts producing fruit.

Being used by the Spirit is first and foremost about surrendering control, but it's also a movement and action toward serving. If you want to discover gifts for service that God has given you, then start serving. That's right—get to work! Start by finding some opportunities with your church body where you can serve on a regular basis. Your serving will grow you, and how God has wired you will begin to surface. This week talk to a pastor at your church and explain that you want to serve—anywhere. Ask him or her to place you in a role he or she sees that best fits who you are.

Day 1

The Holy Spirit Transforms

Encounter the Word

Read Acts 9:1-19.

Explore the Word

Before: Saul was breathing out murderous threats, wanting to imprison anyone who belonged to this Jewish sect called "the Way." He was an educated and zealous follower of Judaism, proud in his heritage as a Jew and willing to do anything it took to keep Judaism pure and undefiled by these new teachings of the rabbi Jesus. The followers of "the Way" and the teachings of Jesus were enemies.

After: Saul, who changed his name to Paul, was speaking in a synagogue, pleading with people. "The Way," he said, "is true. Jesus is the Christ, the Messiah who came from God." For Paul, the teachings of Jesus offered life, and everyone needed to hear about it.

What was the difference? What brought about such an incredible change? *He had encountered the Holy Spirit.*

When you and I encounter the Holy Spirit, we can't help but be changed. "If anyone is in Christ, he is a new creation; the old has gone, the new has come!" (2 Corinthians 5:17). Think about that truth. You have hope for healing today. You have hope for restoration today. The places in your life that are broken can begin to be mended!

Live the Word

Take a few moments to let this new reality sink in. You may want to go look in the mirror, saying to yourself, "You're a new creation; the old has gone, the new has come!"

Day 2

Trusting the Holy Spirit

Encounter the Word

Read Acts 9:20-31.

Explore the Word

Because of the change to his new beliefs and preaching about Jesus, the Jews are trying to kill Paul. At the same time, the community of Christ's followers rejects Paul's change of heart as a counterfeit. After all, he was out to lock them up just a short while before. Paul is caught in the middle, as neither community offers him a place of belonging.

There are two facts that I find fascinating. First, no matter what, Paul continues to speak boldly. It doesn't matter if the Jews are trying to kill him. It doesn't matter if other Christ followers don't believe his transformation to be authentic—he continues to respond to the Holy Spirit.

Second, the community of Christ's followers listens to what the Holy Spirit says through Barnabas about Paul. We have the benefit of reading Acts 9:1-19, but the followers did not. Everything within their natural mind was telling them to not believe that he could change. But believe the Holy Spirit they did. And believe the Holy Spirit *he* did.

Live the Word

What have you been hearing from the Holy Spirit lately? Is there some action He's asking you to take? Is there someone He's asking you to reach out to? Write it on a 3 x 5 card, and keep it with you. Every time you look at it, remind yourself to trust, to believe—and then act.

Day 3

The Holy Spirit Heals

Encounter the Word

Read Acts 9:32-43.

Explore the Word

Think back eight years in your life. What has transpired in your life over the past eight years? What has changed about you? What has changed about our world?

I can't help but think of what it must have been like for Aeneas. For eight years he had been paralyzed. For the past eight years, he had been lying on his back, with no hope of ever walking again. I wonder what was going through his mind that day—the day Peter came to his town, Lydda.

"Jesus Christ heals you. Get up and take care of your mat" (v. 34). Immediately he got up.

Healing. Wholeness. Life. Freedom. The eight years? All in the past. There was a new reality in his life. He was whole. The eight years were finally over.

What have you been waiting for? What have you been praying for? Has it been a long time? Eight years, maybe? Don't worry—just wait. Wait for God's Holy Spirit.

Live the Word

Is there something you've been waiting for and praying for? Write whatever it is on one side of a 3 x 5 card. On the other side of the write down the reference "Acts 9:32-35." Bring it to your next small-group meeting, and give it to someone, asking him or her to join you in praying for whatever it is.

Day 4

The Holy Spirit Hears

Encounter the Word

Read Acts 10:1-23.

Explore the Word

Do you really believe that God hears you?

When you pray, is it just a spiritual exercise, or does it really matter? Does God truly listen to everyone's prayers? Does He listen to *your* prayers?

What we believe about how God hears and answers prayer will affect how we actually live out our prayer life. How would your prayers change if you *knew* that God was really listening?

Today's reading reminds us of a powerful reality—He *is* listening.

Cornelius was a centurion, a military commander. The text adds that he was "devout and God-fearing" (v. 2). It also notes that "he gave generously to those in need." So far, so good. Notice what comes next: he "prayed to God regularly." Cornelius was not Jewish; he was a Gentile (with no connection to God's chosen people, the Israelites). Yet he feared God and followed God, attaching himself to the God of Israel. He did what God desired— "to act justly and to love mercy and to walk humbly with your God" (Micah 6:8).

One day at about three in the afternoon, his whole world changed. An angel appeared to him and said, "Your prayers and gifts to the poor have come up as a memorial offering before God."

God was listening.

How do you think this changed his prayers in the future?

How would your prayers change if you *knew* that God was listening?

Live the Word

Go for a walk. Take a few minutes to look around and smell the outdoors. Maybe go to a park. Find a place where you can be alone. Take a few minutes to talk with God, being honest and real. Tell Him what you're thinking, what you've been feeling lately. Talk to Him as if He were there with you, listening. *Believe* He is listening. He is, you know.

How did that feel? How did that change the way you prayed? What did you sense about God from your time in prayer? Try this exercise weekly for a while; see what kinds of changes it brings about in your prayer time with God.

Day 5

Dignity in the Holy Spirit

Encounter the Word

Read Acts 10:24-48.

Explore the Word

Who is it for you? Maybe it's the man on the street corner holding a sign. Maybe it's the woman with four kids on welfare. Maybe it's someone of another color or race. Who is it for you?

Who is it in your life that you see as "unclean"? You may not use that word to describe it, but who is it that you shy away from for one reason or another? Who is it that you choose not to associate with because they're different, or maybe it's even painful and stressful to be around them?

In today's reading, we encounter Peter about to learn the lesson of a lifetime. Up to this point there was a societal strain between Jews and Gentiles. Jews did not particularly associate with Gentiles, and Gentiles did likewise with Jews. They did not get along well, if at all.

God specifically wanted to deal with the issue, so He came to Peter in a dream and reminded him that all God's creatures have worth and dignity and that none should be called "unclean." God shows no partiality toward or against anyone, and neither should any of us.

Every person on the face of the planet is made in the image of God and has worth and dignity as a human being. There's something of the divine that lives within all of us. The homeless man and the corporate executive—all have identical dignity before their Creator. Peter sums it up well by stating, "I now realize how true it is that God does not show favoritism but accepts men from every nation who fear him and do what is right" (Acts 10:34-35).

The question remains: who is "unclean" to you? Who do you look at and struggle to see the worth that God sees? Who do you have a difficult time treating them as God treats you?

Live the Word

Take a bold step today. Find a way of reaching out to someone you see as "unclean." Make a decision to serve that person in some way today. Don't make it a forced, token act that will put that person on the spot or make them feel uncomfortable. Pray that God will help you to make a natural, genuine gesture of loving-kindness toward them. Ask God for His help to see that person as He sees him or her, as you reach out with an intentional act of service.

Entering In #6
Transformation

Contemplation

When you and I are saturated in the Holy Spirit, we are transformed—changed into something completely different. Old ways of thinking, old ways of living, old values, old habits—all are changed somehow. They are not as attractive anymore. They hold less power over us. Something new, something fresh and alive has come.

All this week in our texts we've encountered various people from different walks of life who share one thing in common: they encountered the Holy Spirit and were changed. One was changed spiritually (Paul). One was changed physically (Aeneas). One was changed mentally (Peter), in their way of thinking. All three encountered the Holy Spirit's transformational power and in a moment were changed forever.

The hope for you and me is this: transformation and change are real possibilities in our lifetime. Spiritually, physically, mentally, socially—whatever it may be—you and I have the possibility of being changed by the Holy Spirit.

Are there broken places in your life? Are you in need of change? Do you need healing in some aspect of your life? Do you have the hope of restoration through the Holy Spirit?

Communication

Take some time to reflect on the truth of God's transformational power in the Holy Spirit. The following are some verses that can help your meditation.

- Ezekiel 11:18-20
- Ezekiel 36:24-28
- Romans 12:1-2
- 2 Corinthians 3:18
- 2 Corinthians 5:16-17

Art and writing are ways for us to express our thoughts and feelings to God in a creative format. They allow us to slow down and think about the subject, finding new and expressive ways of communicating truth. Take a few minutes to create a piece of art or writing through one of the following avenues.

- Draw a picture that represents one of the verses above.
- Write a poem about your own or someone else's transformation.
- Write a letter to God, expressing your heart and your need for transformation in an area of your life, or thanking Him for transforming you.
- Try some other art form you enjoy—painting, music, computer graphic design, photography—whatever helps you express your thoughts and heart.

Community

Whatever avenue of expression you choose, bring that with you to your next small-group time, and share it with your group. Read the verses and enjoy each other's creative expressions of transformation.

Day 1

No Favorites

Encounter the Word

Read Acts 11:1-18.

Explore the Word

Jews were now beginning to hear of Gentiles (non-Jews)
becoming part of "the Way," this new community of
Jewish-Christ followers. This was shocking, because it
was their understanding that the only way Gentiles
could become a part of this family was by first becoming a Jew. To become a Jew one had to be Torah-obser-
vant (which included following all of the Jewish food
laws that told them what they could and could not eat,
and every male had to be circumcised). God used Peter
and six witnesses to testify that a Gentile could become
a Christ follower without becoming a Jew. This opened
the door—God was no longer going to limit himself to
one chosen people. All people could come to Him without hindrance.

Live the Word

At the time that Luke told this story, the Jewish culture
had known that only Jews were able to be a part of
God's chosen people. For them everyone else was a Gentile, "not good enough." Who do we exclude that God
wants to embrace? Think about what might happen to a
convicted and now-freed rapist who showed up at your
church. Where does he sit? Who talks with him? You see,
sometimes in our minds we form lists of spiritual expec-
tations for people, and it's hard for us to let those go.
Who do you need to receive and accept? Ask the Holy
Spirit to reveal to you the names of those you need to
embrace, accepting and inviting them to God's family.

Day 2
The Holy Spirit Goes Urban

Encounter the Word
Read Acts 11:19-30.

Explore the Word
Fleeing persecution, a small group of Christ followers ends up in Antioch. There were several cities during this period named Antioch, but this Antioch, of Syria, was the most influential. It was the third largest city in Roman Empire, and a thriving port metropolis of commercial, political and spiritual influence. The city was a center for the worship of Daphne (famous in Greek mythology for being Apollo's first love).

Meanwhile, the church grew in Antioch, and Barnabas went to find Paul to get him to come and assist the work. This wicked city was the next place where God sent the Holy Spirit, launching Paul's first mission for the Church. Because of the work of the Spirit in this large city, Antioch was the first place to use the term "Christians," for followers of the Way. The Holy Spirit had gone urban!

Live the Word
Apart from Jerusalem, most of Jesus' ministry and teachings took place in very rural and small towns. The Good News was going out to a larger audience—to all Gentiles and now big cities. When was the last time you went to minister in the city? I don't mean just walking around. I mean starting up conversations with the people who live there, looking at the faces of those on their way to work, spending hours praying over the city. Ask the Holy Spirit to lead you to an opportunity to serve in a city. It could be through your church, with a family member, or even on your own.

Day 3
Awaken From Sleep

Encounter the Word
Read Acts 12:1-19.

Explore the Word
Herod Agrippa came from a family of rulers named Herod, who were very famous for their evil ways, especially against the Church. He was disliked by the Jews but he needed their approval politically. So he persecuted the Christ followers in order to gain favor with the Jews. He had Peter put into prison, guarded with 16 soldiers, and chained to two of those soldiers, one on each arm. Once again, it was a great opportunity for God to be glorified. The angel struck Peter on the side, released his chains, opened the doors, and walked him right out. Peter came to himself and realized that it wasn't a dream and walked home to find the community of believers praying for him.

Live the Word
It's interesting to hear Christians talk about how they would love to be around when God did these types of miracles. I've wondered, *Why don't these things happen anymore?* Yet they do. They happen all the time. The Holy Spirit is the same as He's always been and is on the same mission He was sent to do since the resurrection of Jesus. I believe the problem is that we've fallen spiritually asleep. Often God must strike us on the side to open our heart's "eyes" for us to see what's most important. Take some time to ask the Holy Spirit to awaken your eyes, ears, and mind to miracles He's done for you and the miracles He's doing right now in and around your life.

Day 4

The Holy Spirit Glorifies Only One

Encounter the Word

Read Acts 12:19-25.

Explore the Word

Herod's life had been full of evil, deceit, murders, and the pursuit of power. He had dedicated his life in building his own reputation and pride. The people of Tyre and Sidon had not been on good terms with Herod, but a food shortage had occurred, and they wanted to gain his favor in these hard times. He met with them and the people shouted, "This is a voice of a god, not a man" (v. 22). Herod loved this moment, one that perhaps he had dreamed of in his evil heart. However there's only one God, and He's a jealous God. Herod had no place in receiving such praise, but he did nothing to correct the people who uttered it. Instead, he took the opportunity to gloat in what he had accomplished. At that moment God dealt harshly with him by striking him with worms that literally ate him alive!

Live the Word

Listen to God's words in Isaiah 42:8, "I am GOD. That's my name. I don't franchise my glory, don't endorse the no-god idols" (TM). God glorifies himself by placing the Holy Spirit in a believer's life, and that person glorifies Him with their life and service. Read Psalm 139. Take out a journal or some paper, and list all your possessions, anything you have accomplished, anything you hope to do, and all that you are. Then give God praise and credit for all of it. Tell someone else of what God has done for you and through you.

Day 5

The Holy Spirit Reveals Truth

Encounter the Word

Read Acts 13:1-12.

Explore the Word

As the believers were praying in Antioch, they heard the Holy Spirit calling Barnabas and Saul for a missionary journey. You might not have caught that: "the Holy Spirit said" (v. 2). He speaks! They sailed to Cyprus and met with a Roman official who wanted to know more of Jesus. The problem was that his attendant was a sorcerer who opposed this message and tried to convince his boss not to believe. Paul rebuked the sorcerer, who immediately went blind. This was an obvious sign to the official, and he believed.

Live the Word

How do you know when something is true? The only way is to measure it with other known truth. In other words, if I said, "I'm 10 feet tall," you could easily test that against a standard—a tape measure.

How do you know what's spiritually true? If we follow this same logic, we must find a standard measure of truth, such as God's Word, the Bible (which has been a standard of truth for centuries and for millions of people). Read 2 Timothy 3:1-9. There are many false teachers out there who claim some belief or truth, but do not have that power, the Holy Spirit, residing in their life. What time do you invest in knowing the truth in the Bible? Take out a day planner or a week schedule, and map out what your life looks like in a week. See what you could replace to invest more in knowing God's truth.

Entering In #7

Conversation

Contemplation

Let's pray. In other words, let's take this moment to talk to God, and then let's say amen and continue whatever else we're doing. Do you think God would be pleased if our prayers were only asking for things we don't have? Think about it—what would it be like to have a friend you talked to only right before you ate, or when you needed protection? How would that friend feel? How long would he or she stick around? Rest assured that God is not going to leave us—but we are in a relationship, not just asking a "genie in a bottle" to grant our wishes. God wants us to talk with Him always, to be in an ongoing conversation with Him because He is always with us!

Communication

When prayer becomes our foundation for living, we awaken and witness God's amazing work through the Holy Spirit. What's your prayer life like? Take some time to read through how much prayer was a foundation in the Book of Acts. Read through the following verses in Acts: 1:14, 24, 42; 3:1; 4:23-24, 31; 6:4, 6; 7:59; 8:15, 22, 24; 9:11, 40; 10:2, 9, 30-31; 11:5; 12:5, 12; 13:3; 14:23; 16:13, 16, 25; 20:36; 21:5; 22:17; 26:29; 27:29; 28:8.

Prayer is conversation with your Creator. One other aspect of prayer that's often overlooked is praying or talking with the Holy Spirit. God is "three in One": Father, Son, and Holy Spirit. Since we talk to God and Jesus in prayer, why not the Holy Spirit? It might feel awkward at first, so begin to pray to the Holy Spirit this week as you think of Him. Ask Him for guidance and patience or whatever else you might need.

Compassion

Once prayer has become a natural part of your day, you will begin to realize that God's presence is always with you. You can talk with Him and praise Him for the big and small things in your life. You will see the Father as a loving, caring Creator, and if you're practicing your conversations with the Holy Spirit, you will begin to realize His role as the Helper. As you grow in your prayer life, begin to focus on prayers that are beyond yourself. Pray for others, pray for your city, your friends, family, neighbors, and any other person or situation of which you are aware. Pray at the moment you learn of it.

Day 1

Defining Success

Encounter the Word

Read Acts 13:13-52.

Explore the Word

In Pisidian Antioch, Paul and Barnabas were invited to the synagogue to speak to the Jews. As happened before, the Holy Spirit again gave Paul a speech proclaiming the work of God from the past to the present including His Son, Jesus. Word got out, and the next week, crowds of Gentiles came to hear about God. This caused some Jews to be jealous and bitter, so they ran Paul and Barnabas's out of the region.

Live the Word

Look at the last two verses: 51 and 52. In the Jewish culture Jews would often shake off the dust from their feet when they were in Gentile cities. When they did this they were showing their desire to be separate from the Gentiles. So imagine the shock when Paul and Barnabas did this to show their separation from a community of fellow Jews! Then it says in verse 52 that "They were filled with joy and the Holy Spirit." It sounds odd, doesn't it? Was this ministry a success or a failure? Here's the key: Paul and Barnabas knew that they were responsible to obediently proclaim the message—no matter what the outcome. Are there people you know who don't believe in Jesus Christ? Your role is to simply live obediently. Take some time to think of those who don't know Jesus. Offer them up to God, and ask the Holy Spirit to lead them to Christ.

Day 2

The Holy Spirit Divides

Encounter the Word

Read Acts 14:1-7.

Explore the Word

In Iconium, Paul and Barnabas found a great response of belief to the message of truth. However, the city was divided, and those who chose not to believe stirred up resistance. Paul and Barnabas kept working, and the Holy Spirit gave them power to do miraculous works to confirm the truth of all that they were saying. Still, the Jews who didn't believe were "poisoning the minds" of the Gentiles. Once again, where there is a great movement of God there will also be evil there to resist it. This group of jealous Jewish leaders got some of the Gentiles to develop a plan to kill Paul and Barnabas. So Paul and Barnabas eventually left this growing ministry to follow the Holy Spirit to another place.

Live the Word

Following Jesus is not easy. Paul and Barnabas left home to share about Jesus, only to be argued with, expelled, pelted with rocks, and nearly killed. I sometimes wonder how many of us would have quit. How many of us couldn't handle the rejection and division? Following Jesus is hard, and because of that it will divide people. People must choose, and sometimes they will choose not to believe. The question is, will we still share Christ's love when it is difficult? Take some time to get away and settle this issue—whether or not you will you continue to follow Jesus even when it gets tough. Pray through that, and then pray for friends and family members, that they would join you.

Day 3
The Holy Spirit Demands a Response

Encounter the Word
Read Acts 14:8-20.

Explore the Word
Here is a man crippled from birth, who had never walked. The Lord healed him through the ministry of Paul. Obviously this generated much attention to the point that many believed Paul and Barnabas to be Greek gods. This caused the priests of Zeus to come to offer a sacrifice to them. This was exactly opposite of what Paul and Barnabas wanted to see happen! The situation escalated when some Jews from Antioch and from Iconium, who expelled them from their cities, saw the pagan sacrifices being offered and began stirring up the crowd against them. These Jews won over the crowd, and Paul was dragged out of the city and hit with rocks until they thought he was dead.

Live the Word
You have to choose. Paul had to choose whether he would be fully obedient and face whatever came his way. The people had to choose who they would believe. Listen to the writer of Hebrews: "So let's keep at it and eventually arrive at the place of rest, not drop out through some sort of disobedience. . . . His powerful Word is sharp as a surgeon's scalpel, cutting through everything, whether doubt or defense, laying us open to listen and obey. Nothing and no one is impervious to God's Word. We can't get away from it—no matter what" (4:11-13, TM). God's Word demands that we respond. We either obey or we don't. Memorize these verses this week so that the Holy Spirit may bring them to mind later, when you are discouraged and thinking about giving up.

Day 4

The Holy Spirit on a Mission

Encounter the Word

Read Acts 14:21-28.

Explore the Word

Paul and Bárnabas eventually returned to Antioch of Syria, the "big" Antioch where Paul first started. Their journey had been a success despite the persecution. They started many churches throughout their journey, and Paul would eventually write a letter (the Book of Galatians) to the churches within the area of Galatia. The letter dealt with much of the resistance from the "Judaizers" (the ones who thought people had to become Jews before they could become followers of Jesus) and called them to faith and freedom in Christ. Before arriving at their home port of Antioch, Paul and Barnabas quickly retraced their steps through Lystra, Iconium, and Antioch (the small one) to appoint key leaders (called elders) at each stop.

Live the Word

What is the goal of the Holy Spirit? We know for one that He is the transformer of our lives, but what does He want to do with us? Read 2 Timothy 2:2. The Holy Spirit is on a mission to build the Church. When you stop and think about this mission, you quickly realize that He is not about gathering a super group of disciples all together so they can only invest in each other. Rather, He scatters them to affect others. The Holy Spirit is on this mission that's mobile—it's on the move. We're a part of something that leaves the safety of community to change the world. Read the mission statement of Matthew 28:19-20 and memorize it. Ask God to give you boldness to respond in obedience to the Holy Spirit's call on your life.

The Holy Spirit's Ministry of Grace

Encounter the Word

Read Acts 15:1-21.

Explore the Word

Paul and Barnabas were in sharp disagreement with a group of Jewish Christians called the "Judaizers." This group believed in Jesus but could not see Gentiles coming into the family without strictly following the law of Moses. The council in Jerusalem became the ruling body for most of the churches at this time. Even though there were no official church structures like we see today, Jerusalem was seen as the mother church. Because of its strong Jewish culture and connection to the Temple, the Jerusalem church had deep roots in the law of Moses. This group of Judaizers ultimately wanted a distinction between Jewish believers and Gentile believers. What they wanted was to essentially take a step back from where God was heading—to take the Temple curtain and sew it back shut. They wanted to ensure that the connection to God through the Jews be reinstated.

The council of Jerusalem focused on the ritual of circumcision and whether it was necessary for Gentile believers to be circumcised before they could become followers of Jesus. Peter made his speech, which told of the Holy Spirit filling and empowering Gentile believers, without them having to follow Jewish laws and practices first. His speech indicated that God had removed any difference between Jews and Gentiles, and that the burden of the law had been lifted for good. In other words, God gave the Gentiles grace—making them right before Him without having to "earn" their righteousness through the

Jewish law. Grace means getting something that we don't deserve. Our faith in Christ is based on God's grace. Any other message preached is false. We did not earn our faith—we received it as a gift.

Live the Word

Have you ever lost your equilibrium? That's when you're so dizzy that you can't tell which end is up. It happens a lot under water or on airplanes. It can happen spiritually as well. We lose our spiritual equilibrium when we're out of fellowship with other strong believers and not filling our lives with God's truth from the Scriptures. In the air they always say, "Look at your instruments," and that's a good rule for our spiritual lives —keep an eye on the "gauge of grace." What is the measure of grace in your faith? Are you living your life by it? Are you trying to earn favor with God through good performance? Or have you decided to receive the righteousness God gives freely through Christ—by His grace? Are you sharing that same grace with others? Take some time to drop to your knees and thank God for the grace He has given you.

Entering In #8

Sending

Contemplation

I love spy movies. I'm drawn to the mystery and suspense, but I'm intrigued the most by the secret missions. The agent gets a top-secret envelope and opens it to read a message detailing his or her next assignment. The agent packs up, leaves loved ones, skips the celebrations, and takes off.

At the end of my boot camp basic training in the Marine Corps we had a similar scenario. Hundreds of us newly trained soldiers were handed envelopes that gave us our official assignments. Some of us would become military police, some cooks, some pilots, and some mechanics. All of us would have different missions, would be sent in different directions, and very possibly never see each other again. That was the nature of receiving an assignment. You got your orders, and no matter how your life changed once you got that envelope, you dropped everything and took off to follow them.

Is it possible that we as believers today have a mixed-up perspective on what following Christ looks like? How often do we hand God *our* envelope of orders? How often do we pray for guidance wishing God would just hand us an envelope—make His will plain—but really the envelope is right there in front of us, we're just afraid to take it? In our readings this week we see that Paul is launched out by the Holy Spirit on his second missionary journey. He and Barnabas will make stops for days or weeks at a time, but they will always be sent somewhere else. You see, God is not in the business of trying to keep Christians huddled up—He is about *sending us out.*

Communication

Could you imagine living Paul's life? He was always being sent somewhere, to care for the new believers there, and then leaving for a new place of opportunity. In Matthew 9:37-38 Jesus said, "The harvest is plentiful but the workers are few. Ask the Lord of the harvest, therefore, to send out workers into his harvest field." Sending is a large part of what it means to be a Christian. God sends His Son, the Son sends the Holy Spirit, and the Holy Spirit sends us.

Community

Where are you being sent? You might not ever get a secret military envelope, but you *will* be prompted by the Holy Spirit. He calls those who are fully surrendered to Him and ready. Look at it this way: if I finished boot camp and never received my mission, never received my orders, what use would I have been? A lot of Christians have received their leading from the Holy Spirit to be sent—but never go. We have to go. We're a part of God's master plan to send us out to seek and save the lost so that one day we will all be with Him forever.

This week begin to look at your current role in life. Look at this idea of "being sent" in a different way. Our "sending" has already happened for many of us, and it's right where we live. You've been sent to the family you were given. You've been sent to the school you attend. You've been sent to live by the neighbors you have. What if this is your mission? Pray for those around you this week, and look differently at the people and places you have been placed near. See them as those who need to hear the Good News of the love of God and look for the ways you can share that love with them.

Day 1

Holy Spirit Wisdom

Encounter the Word
Read Acts 15:22-35.

Explore the Word
In Acts 15, the community of Christ followers were struggling with some people who were going around promoting beliefs that were hindering Gentiles from connecting with Christ. These people were saying that Gentile believers needed to be circumcised and obey the law of Moses to be saved. The community needed guidance, so they sought God.

After meeting together, they decided to write the letter that we have in verses 23-29. The hallmark of the letter is the words "It seemed good to the Holy Spirit and to us" (v. 28). When in need of guidance, the community of followers went to the source, the leadership of the Holy Spirit. They remembered the promise of Jesus in John 16:13, where He reminded them, "But when he, the Spirit of truth, comes, he will guide you into all truth."

Live the Word
In what area are you in need of guidance? Before your next small-group time, make a note of one area where you are seeking guidance. Share that area at your next small group, asking them to join with you in prayer over that area. Make a master list for every person in your group, detailing areas where they are seeking guidance too. Commit to praying every day for each person. Come back the following week and share any thoughts or leadings from the Holy Spirit that you've been given.

Day 2

Disagreements Under the Spirit

Encounter the Word

Read Acts 15:36-41.

Explore the Word

It's not a matter of "if" we will encounter disagreements, but "when" we will encounter disagreements. The question is: how will we handle them? We can choose to deal with them in a straightforward, godly manner, leading to some form of resolution, or we can deal with them in a manner that leaves wounds and pain in others.

Paul and Barnabas disagreed over taking John Mark with them on their upcoming second missionary journey. Barnabas thought it was a good idea; Paul didn't. Paul still remembered how John Mark had deserted them in Pamphylia during their first missionary journey (Acts 13:13). We don't know the reasons for John Mark's leaving, nor are we given a full picture of how Paul and Barnabas resolved their differences. One thing we do know is that God used what seemed to be a bad situation and turned it into a positive—there were now two missionary teams being sent out instead of one.

Live the Word

Look up the following verses from the Book of Proverbs: 12:18; 13:10; 14:29; 15:1; 16:20; 16:28; 18:8; 18:21; 19:20.

What does each say about disagreements and our words?

Day 3

Guided by the Holy Spirit

Encounter the Word

Read Acts 16:1-15.

Explore the Word

Notice what is happening in verses 6, 7, and 10. They had been kept by the Holy Spirit . . . They tried to enter . . . but the Spirit of Jesus would not let them . . . After Paul had seen the vision, we got ready to leave. . . .

I stand back and wonder sometimes, *God, why don't I see You intimately involved around me?* The Holy Spirit guided Paul, telling him where to go at every turn. Why don't I see the Holy Spirit guiding my life that way? The Holy Spirit is just as active in our lives as He was in Paul's life. He's still about the same mission. So what's the difference?

Sometimes it's our busyness. We can't hear the Holy Spirit's promptings because we can't hear Him over the din of the noise in our lives. Our lives are spent on the pursuit of so many things that we're crowding him out. If we don't consciously slow down and seek His voice, we'll never afford Him the space He needs to speak and lead in our lives.

Live the Word

Take a day to unplug from the electronic noise in your life. Don't listen to any music. Don't watch television. Don't play any video games. Allow silence into your soul. Slow down, and continually ask God to speak into your life all day long. At the end of the day, record what you heard from God. How did the Holy Spirit speak to you today? How did He lead you?

Day 4

The Holy Spirit Perspective

Encounter the Word

Read Acts 16:16-40.

Explore the Word

Most of us run our situations in life through a certain filter. Everything that happens to us is labeled "good" or "bad," mostly corresponding to the direct impact it has on our lives. God doesn't see our lives through that filter. He is not concerned with how "good" we feel but is ultimately concerned as to how situations will shape us for our true good and form us more and more into His likeness.

Take today's text, for example. Our self-centered filter would label jail—"bad." Yet Paul and Silas were praying and singing hymns to God in jail at midnight—they had a transformed perspective on life.

We're never promised that our lives will be easy. We're never promised that everything in our lives can be labeled "good." But one thing is for sure: once you and I are filled with the Holy Spirit, it doesn't matter anymore.

Live the Word

- As you survey your life, what are some situations going on right now that you need the Holy Spirit to help you relabel?
- Consider the fact that Paul and Silas did not know the outcome of Acts 16:16-40. They did not know how or if God would show up in a miraculous way. What can you learn from this text about your perspective on the trials that come your way?

Day 5

No Middle Ground

Encounter the Word

Read Acts 17:1-9.

Explore the Word

Paul and his companions had now arrived in Thessalonica, the principal city of Macedonia. Once again they went to the local synagogue, where Paul talked about Jesus through the Old Testament scriptures. Paul convincingly argued that Jesus, the rabbi from Nazareth, was in fact the Christ. His message stirred people. Some were persuaded and joined them as Christ followers, but there were others who did not. Those Jews who disagreed with Paul organized a mob and started a riot in the city. They were jealous over the fact that their "faithful" were leaving them and joining themselves to this new teaching from Paul.

Whenever God is at work, there's going to be opposition. Speak out about your beliefs, and some will agree and some won't. Stand for what's right, and you'll find those who applaud you and those who won't. Live your life as a Christ follower, and you'll find people who resonate with your life and those who find it foreign. There seems to be no middle ground when it comes to the Holy Spirit. Why is it that we try to live as if there were?

Live the Word

Take a quick survey through the Book of Acts. Write down all the times Christ followers faced opposition. What can you learn from each of those instances? How does what you've read reinforce or speak to you about the countercultural nature of being a Christ follower?

Entering In #9
Proclamation

Contemplation

The minute anyone mentions your favorite movie, what happens? "Did you see that movie? It was incredible." Even the retelling of a great movie is exciting.

The curtain opens on the Book of Acts with Jesus making a statement that sets the tone for the entire Book of Acts: "You will receive power when the Holy Spirit comes on you; and you will be my witnesses in Jerusalem, and in all Judea and Samaria, and to the ends of the earth" (Acts 1:8). In effect, Jesus was saying, "This story you've seen and been changed by—go tell it. Go live it with others. Go and connect others to the story." And Acts chronicles many such "retellings."

Scanning through the pages of Acts, it becomes apparent that there was no formula, no "four steps to storytelling" given. There was no "one right way" to share the message with people. Most just spoke what the Holy Spirit laid on their hearts to say.

Communication

Although there was no formula, there are some common threads that begin to emerge in the pages of Acts. Look for these as you continue to read the story of Acts.

- Proclamation (or retelling) happens in ordinary moments—moments orchestrated by God, not by His followers.

- Proclamation is a verbal account of God: who He is and what He has done in the here and now. The message is focused on Jesus and the Kingdom, not on feelings but on the truth of the story.

- Proclamation is not about giving answers but about announcing truth. It's great to remember that we don't have to know all the answers to share the message.

- Proclamation is not about "selling something." It's about entering into a conversation with someone. It takes time, sometimes years. Conversation is as much about listening as it is about talking.

- The Holy Spirit is the One who brings the results, not the reteller. It's not up to you to "get people saved." God is the One who rescues and restores.

- Some will respond to the message; others will not. For those who truly believe and truly respond, a genuine transformation occurs.

Community

Be sure to talk through the list above at your next small-group time. Discuss how those truths impact you and what you've been taught about "evangelism." How are they the same? How are they revolutionary?

At the conclusion of your group time, have each person identify someone he or she can enter into conversation with—retelling the story to them. Pray for each person in the group and the person he or she wants to engage in conversation. Begin that conversation this week, and report what happened.

Day 1

The Words of the Holy Spirit

Encounter the Word
Read Acts 17:10-15.

Explore the Word
"How sweet are your words to my taste, sweeter than honey to my mouth!" (Psalm 119:103).

Typical Hebrews loved the Scriptures. It was something that was formed within them from early on. Starting at the age of 6 through the age of 10, young boys and girls started to memorize the Torah (the first five books of the Bible). They saturated themselves in the ancient texts. From the ages of 10 to 14, boys would memorize the rest of the Hebrew Bible (all the way to Malachi), while the girls would memorize the psalms and the prophets. At the age of 14, Jewish boys would apply to become a *talmidim,* or a disciple of a rabbi, and would memorize the major *midrash,* or rabbinic interpretations of the Hebrew Bible.

A love of the ancient text was ingrained in them. In fact, every time they read from the Torah scroll in the synagogue (of which Paul was certainly a witness and partaker), whoever was to read from it would carry it into the assembly, dancing with it as people reached out to touch and kiss it. No doubt Jesus and Paul, who both read from the Torah scroll, had danced with it as well.

The Hebrew mindset was saturated with a love for the Scriptures.

It shouldn't be odd, then, to find the description in Acts 17:11, applied to the Jews of Berea. It says that they were people who "examined the Scriptures every day to see if what Paul said was true." They were in line with the great tradition of the Hebrew people, who loved the text, lived for the text, breathed in the text, and savored the text.

What about us? Do we truly love the Scriptures? Do we live in the Scriptures? Do we breathe in the God's word for us? Do we deeply savor His instruction?

To do any less would be to deny its life and power.

Live the Word

Read Psalm 19:7-11 through a few times. Allow the words of the text to pour over you as a waterfall. Read it silently. Read it aloud. Read it slowly, focusing on every word.

Now take out a piece of paper and rewrite Psalm 19:7-11 in your own words, making it as personal to you as you like. Take that piece of paper and hang it in a prominent place, where you will see it often and be reminded of the words you've written. You may even want to memorize this passage as a way of solidifying those ancient words in your soul.

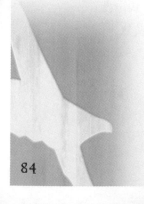

Day 2

Broken by the Spirit

Encounter the Word

Read Acts 17:16-34.

Explore the Word

None of us wants to be broken. Brokenness implies that something needs to be fixed, it is damaged beyond usefulness. It implies that our efforts at "keeping it all together" have failed.

Yet in God's economy, brokenness is the first step in the process of transformation. We need to be broken. Brokenness brings healing. Brokenness reminds us that we're dependent on Him. It places us in a realm where the Holy Spirit can move and operate in our lives.

God longs to break your heart with the things that break His. He longs to take your hardened heart and break it so that it's soft and moldable.

Acts 17:16 reminds us that upon entering Athens, Paul was "greatly distressed to see that the city was full of idols." His heart was moved; it was broken over what he saw—the spiritual poverty of the great city of Athens. His heart broke with the things that broke the heart of the Holy Spirit.

When was the last time the Holy Spirit broke you? When was the last time you were broken for the needs of those around you? Has it been too long?

Live the Word

Read the following passages, allowing the words to fill your soul:

- Psalm 34:18

- Psalm 51:17
- Isaiah 61:1-3
- Ezekiel 21:6-7
- Matthew 5:3

Paul was broken by what he saw in Athens. The Holy Spirit led him to action. What has the Holy Spirit been breaking your heart with lately? What will you do about it?

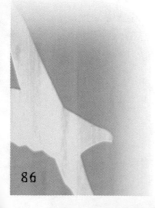

Day 3

Encouragement from the Spirit

Encounter the Word

Read Acts 18:1-17.

Explore the Word

The Church today lives in what many have called a "fortress" mentality. It's the idea that in the raging sea of culture today, the Church needs to be a rock of security for people. It needs to be a place where people can find refuge from the storms of life, safe shelter from the wind and waves. It sounds good. But think about it.

The Church is not a place—it's people. It resides in the hearts and souls of followers as they gather together, wherever that may be. The Church was never meant to be a "fortress" but it was meant to be a gathering of Christ followers, who are involved in a countercultural, subversive Kingdom movement. The Church doesn't exist to preserve the goodness of its people, sheltering them from the world. It exists for the people outside of it, those not yet a part of that gathering. It is a light to them, and one of the primary means God uses to reach them.

Our text for today reminds us of God's agenda for this world. He comes to Paul in a vision in the middle of the night saying, "Don't be afraid. Don't run away into a bubble. Keep on interacting with the lost. Keep on speaking. Don't run away from them. Don't be silent. I know it would be easy to do just that—but what about the lost? Who will go to them?"

Who *will* go to them if we run and hide, safe within the walls of our "fortress"?

Paul took courage and "stayed a year and a half, teaching them the word of God" (Acts 18:11).

Don't be afraid. Don't run away from your lost friends. Talk to them. Spend time with them. Because if you run away and hide, who will go to them?

Live the Word

Who in your sphere of life needs to know about the teachings of Jesus? Rather than wait and pray for someone to reach out to him or her, why don't you? Start a conversation today with that person—not a monologue—only telling him or her what you believe. Listen. Ask the person what he or she thinks about God. Find out about his or her thoughts on church and "Christians." If you ask and listen, you may be amazed. Evangelism is not simply about "telling" but about entering into a spiritual dialogue with those around you. Begin that conversation today.

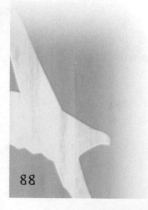

Day 4

The Holy Spirit in Ephesus

Encounter the Word

Read Acts 18:18-28.

Explore the Word

Ephesus was the world center of Artemis worship. She was known as "the many-breasted one," referring to the statue of Artemis, which represented her role as the goddess of fertility, childbirth, and perpetual virginity (quite a paradox). During that time almost half of the women of Ephesus died in childbirth, so to worship the goddess of childbirth was essential. The thought was that if you worshiped Artemis, then you would be protected in childbirth.

The worship of Artemis was big business. Millions of statues of her likeness were made and sold. In fact, one of the most lucrative jobs in all of Ephesus was being a silversmith who made silver statues of Artemis. Every year after winter the port was opened, and the whole city would parade the statue of Artemis through the streets to the port, where they would dip it into the water to bless the merchant vessels.

Worship of Artemis was central to the life of the Ephesians. A temple was built to the goddess there. It was known as a place of social welfare for local citizens, a place of assistance for travelers, a place of cultural influence through the arts and music, and a place where thinkers and creators would gather. The temple even functioned as a sort of a bank or financial institution, offering loans and selling land to local citizens.

Ephesus was perhaps the largest pagan worshiping center in the known world at the time. It is into this arena that we find Paul and his companions going, to speak boldly of the truth of God—the one true God.

Imagine how they must have felt, a small band of travelers entering the massive port city of Ephesus, bringing a message that would threaten the very economic and social structure to the entire city. Seems insurmountable, doesn't it? Yet the amazing truth is that within 30 years Artemis worship was all but gone, and Ephesus had become one of the largest Jesus-worshiping centers in the known world.

Amazing what the Holy Spirit can do when we respond to His leading!

Live the Word

To gain a little more background on Ephesus and Paul, read the first three chapters of Paul's letter to the Ephesians. Be sure to note any interesting comments that Paul makes in reference to what we've already discussed about the city of Ephesus and the worship of Artemis. Look for one verse or paragraph that would help you talk to others about Jesus among the "other gods," and write out what God is teaching you through that passage.

Day 5

The Holy Spirit Impacts a City

Encounter the Word

Read Acts 19:1-22.

Explore the Word

In today's text we read about the Holy Spirit working powerfully through Paul. Together they were having a tremendous impact on the city of Ephesus. Take the rest of your time in study, observing the following:

What is the Holy Spirit doing in Acts 19:1-22?

What is Paul doing in Acts 19:1-22?

What is the response of the people in Acts 19:17-20?

What are some of the results of the activity of the Holy Spirit in the city of Ephesus as mentioned in Acts 19:1-22?

How are these events remarkable given what you've already learned about Ephesus?

Live the Word

Take a few moments to write a letter to God, giving Him praise for what He did in the lives of those who lived in Ephesus. Reflect on the things you've learned over the past few days. How has your vision of God and the Holy Spirit changed? Respond to God over what you've learned. What do you feel God is teaching you, and what do you need to do about it?

Entering In #10

Influence

Contemplation

Athens. Corinth. Ephesus. All three cities were the major metropolitan areas of their region. All three had a major influence in the thinking and culture of the day. Athens was a world center of culture and philosophy. Corinth was a world center of finance and commerce. Ephesus was a world center of pagan worship. And each was influenced by the teachings of one man: Paul.

In the texts we read this week, Paul visits each of these major metropolitan areas, proclaiming the message of God. It's interesting to note how Paul approached each of the cities. In the center of philosophy, he spoke of the "unknown god" in their midst, bringing a new "teaching" (or philosophy). In the center of commerce, he became a tentmaker, earning a living and sharing the message through his trade. In the center of pagan religion, he lectured, and God performed miraculous signs through him, equal to or greater than the pagan gods of the region had ever done.

In his letter to the Corinthian believers, Paul shares his heart: "I have become all things to all men so that by all possible means I might save some" (1 Corinthians 9:22). Paul spoke the language of his day to reach the people of his day. He knew the culture and the times. He used the means of the day to communicate eternal truth.

So it should be with us.

Communication

Before your next small-group meeting, take some time to research one of the three cities Paul visited in this week's texts (Athens, Corinth, or Ephesus). You may want to look in a commentary on the Book of Acts to find more information about the city. You might also want to check in a Bible dictionary or a Bible encyclopedia for more information. The Internet may hold some gems as well. Using a good search engine could lead you to some interesting information.

Community

Be sure to bring all you learned to your small group. Go city by city in your group, allowing people the opportunity to present their findings on the life of the city. Then go back and read Acts 17:16—19:22 as a group. Take time to note where your findings on the city help you understand the text in a new light. How will these new insights change the way you look at your world and sphere of influence?

Day 1

Ministry Has Consequences

Encounter the Word

Read Acts 19:23-41.

Explore the Word

Paul had been in the city of Ephesus for two years teaching and encouraging followers. The Church was growing in that city which had been a thriving pagan worship center for Artemis, the goddess of fertility. The volume of travelers made for big business for the silversmiths, who made the Artemis statues purchased by travelers and locals.

Eventually the silversmith business began feeling the impact of people converting and following Jesus. One silversmith, Demetrius, organized a town meeting that had people from all over the city gathering in its famous 25,000-seat theater. He reminded them that this new religion was crippling business, and stealing glory from Artemis. Showing their loyalty (to the gods and their wallets) they soon began shouting, "Great is Artemis!" But when Paul and his disciples heard this, they didn't run away. They worked together to find the wisest way to respond. They stayed until the Holy Spirit sent them on to another city to be a witness there.

Live the Word

Think about it: an entire city was gathering to riot over those who were telling the story of Jesus. Would *you* have stuck around? Take some time to read other stories in the Scriptures of those who ministered through opposition. (Start with Hebrews 11.) Ask the Holy Spirit to give you courage and boldness so you can respond the same way.

Day 2

Start with Encouragement

Encounter the Word

Read Acts 20:1-12.

Explore the Word

Here we find an instance where Paul encouraged his disciples. This is most likely something he learned from his friend Barnabas, whose name means "encourager." The text says that Paul traveled the area and encouraged people with words. He eventually found his way to Troas, where he spoke until midnight—when a man named Eutychus fell three floors out of a window while listening to Paul and died. The Holy Spirit used Paul to raise him from the dead, which is alarming considering the fact that a miracle like this had not been mentioned or done since the resurrection of Jesus.

Live the Word

Can we ever expect to heal people, let alone raise them from the dead? Is that the right question? Many Christians today focus on the spectacular or the big stuff. Sometimes people aspire to do the "spotlight ministry" in order to feel better about themselves or to feel more powerful. Yet Luke mentioned that Paul's purpose was to encourage people with his words. Read Hebrews 4:12-14. How do you encourage others in their faith? Spiritual encouragement is not just flattery or nice talk, but it is encouraging someone's faith and obedience to Christ. Take out some paper, and list three people you could encourage in their faith. Now use this week to give them those words.

Day 3

A Compelling Call

Encounter the Word

Read Acts 20:13-38.

Explore the Word

Paul continued his mission and sailed for Assos, finally arriving at Miletus, where he sent for the elders in Ephesus to give them some farewell words of encouragement. In Paul's farewell he reminded them of his intentions and set the record straight for why he was on this quest. Here we have an insight into what motivated Paul—he was "compelled by the Spirit" (v. 22). Paul was compelled to obey no matter what lay ahead.

Live the Word

The word "compelled" means to be bound or enslaved to something. In other words, Paul was "bound" to the Holy Spirit, and anything He asked he knew he must do. Paul was saying he had no choice but to obey.

Are you compelled to obey? Are you bound to whatever the Holy Spirit asks of you? This is not something that will be easy; on the contrary, it takes great faith and trust that God will take care of you. Take some time to read through the Psalms, and copy down a Psalm that you can carry with you and read to remind you of His amazing care for you on your journey. (Suggestion: Start with Psalm 95:6-7 and Psalm 55).

Day 4

A New Family

Encounter the Word

Read Acts 21:1-16.

Explore the Word

Despite his driven personality and disciplined lifestyle, Paul was a beloved friend. He had to tear himself away from those he loved in Ephesus to sail on to Tyre. Once again, Luke lets us see the personal connection side of Paul and how he was truly loved by other believers. This picture of Paul, with the leaders of the church, their wives and children all walking to the beach together to say goodbye is a great reminder that the Church is people—husbands, wives, kids, moms, dads, brothers, sisters and friends.

Live the Word

Family—it is the most intimate of words. The word conjures up memories of laughter, tears, adventure, teamwork, and togetherness. In the Scriptures one of the most common metaphors used to describe the relationship between believers is family. I don't know what your family experience is or was like, but I do know that God's promise for our spiritual family is much more than anything we could imagine. As a follower of Christ you're a part of a new family, and God is your loving father. Read the following passages: Psalm 103:1-14; Romans 8:16-18; 2 Corinthians 6:17-18; Ephesians 5:1-2. Reflect on how God sees you and what he wants you to know about your relationship to Him and your new family. Write a note of thanks to Him.

Day 5

The Holy Spirit Prepares Paul

Encounter the Word

Read Acts 21:17-36.

Explore the Word

In the previous passage, a prophet named Agabus gave a prophecy that Paul would be bound and tied by the Jews in Jerusalem. Paul was not surprised and added that he would also die—and yet he still sailed to Jerusalem! The Holy Spirit had given Paul great boldness and courage to face whatever might come.

As a way to win favor with the Jews who opposed him, Paul was asked to take an oath of purity with four other men that would demonstrate a reverence toward the Law of Moses. The oath of purity was called a Nazarite vow. The ceremony would require them to refrain from drinking any wine or strong drink, not to touch or be near any dead person, and not cut their hair for the time of the vow. It was a ceremony and vow of purification. Despite this attempt to win over his opposition, Paul was still arrested.

Live the Word

It's hard for us to blindly obey without any idea of what's ahead. Paul's Nazarite vow was an interesting event that some say was his preparation to be the ultimate sacrifice for God—to die for Him. He was purified and prepared. We might not see life this way, but the Holy Spirit is on a mission to build the Church and also to purify and prepare us as "living sacrifices." Read Rom. 12:1-2 a few times, and ask God continue making your life a pure living sacrifice for Him.

Entering In #11

Compulsion

Contemplation

I'll never forget my first bungee jumping experience. A group of friends decided to drive to the desert and try this new extreme sport. It was a very new idea at the time, and not many people had ever heard of it. So all of us stared at this huge crane in the middle of the desert, laughing and joking—but I was nervous. I'm not fond of heights, but I knew I had to do this. I was bound to this group and to the goal of all of us completing this task.

Have you felt that you just had to do something—that you were meant to do it? It's in that moment your heart is beating fast because you know you were built to do it. You can't free yourself from it. Through Paul's journeys he remained bound to obedience, no matter what came his way. All throughout his journeys and life, Paul responds as though he has no other choice but to follow the Holy Spirit's call.

Communication

Have you ever felt compelled to do something for God? In Acts 20:24 we see how deep this compulsion goes for Paul: "I consider my life worth nothing to me, if only I may finish the race and complete the task the Lord Jesus has given me—the task of testifying to the gospel of God's grace."

Despite not knowing what's ahead except for persecution, he says in essence, "I have no other choice." We need more Christ followers who live this way, compelled to do anything God asks. People bound to obedience, regardless of the cost.

Community

This week determine with your group to begin to listen—not when it's quiet but when it's noisy. When you're right smack in the middle of life, busy, crowded and full of activity, listen for Holy Spirit's compelling call. Whatever it is, you'll know! Your heart will race, and your mind will try to rationalize why you shouldn't—but do it! You're compelled to obey the Creator. Divide up into partners to connect with each other throughout the week and remind each other to be listening.

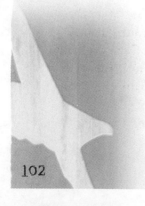

Day 1

Setting the Course

Encounter the Word

Read Acts 21:37—22:29.

Explore the Word

Paul was arrested by the Roman guards and thrown into prison without many questions asked. In those days a Roman law prohibited creating a mob or a riot in the cities. If you did, you could be arrested. Yet the bitter Jewish leaders only cared that their traditions were upheld no matter the cost. Paul was given the chance to address the crowd in his own defense, but his unwavering commitment to preach the truth only increased the crowd's anger and desire for him to be killed. As Paul was about to be flogged, he asked why he had been given no trial. This was important, because no Roman citizen could be flogged without formally being found guilty at a trial.

Live the Word

What an amazing series of events! Paul was expelled, hunted, and stoned in nearly every city he traveled to, and now he was in Roman custody. That means he was protected by the Roman guard, he would travel to Rome in their ships, he would have contact with the highest officials of their cities. What a course that God and the Holy Spirit had put Paul on! There will be many times in life when we might not understand why God is allowing something to happen to us and where He'll have us go next. Our role is not to chart the course but simply to follow where the wind of the Holy Spirit will take us. Take a walk, and ask God to give you patience as you endure tough times in your life.

Day 2

The Holy Spirit Confronts Evil

Encounter the Word

Read Acts 22:30—23:11.

Explore the Word

The next day after the mob scene in Jerusalem, the commander wanted to get to the bottom of why these people were so angry. He had all the chief priests of the Sanhedrin assemble to explain the previous day's events. Paul was struck in the mouth for his words to the Sanhedrin, which leads Paul to respond by calling them "whitewashed walls." The term was used to refer to an old wall that's ready to fall over and is painted to hide its condition. This insult was well understood. These leaders have no goodness in them—it's only painted on.

Live the Word

I'm struck with how bold and sharp Paul was. Yet this was not because Paul was educated and bold but because the Holy Spirit was there giving him the words to say. The Holy Spirit was confronting the evil actions and attitudes of these religious leaders. Do you ever wonder if you could confront evil? Let me answer for you—no, you can't! This is what the Holy Spirit does in and through our lives. The part we play is being in tune with the Holy Spirit so we can hear Him. Again, our problem is usually that we're too busy and full of activities that drown out His voice. Read Mark 13:10-11. This is another chance for you to take that quiet walk in a nature-filled area and listen for the Holy Spirit's voice. You may not hear anything from Him at this time. But practice listening, and enjoy your time with God.

Day 3

Gaining Momentum

Encounter the Word

Read Acts 23:12-35.

Explore the Word

In verse 11 God gave Paul some words of encouragement, telling him that he would be sent to Rome to be a witness for Him. How exciting for Paul, a Roman citizen, to receive a call to preach in the greatest and most powerful city of that time!

The reading for today, however, is quite traumatic. A plot to kill Paul is discovered, and his sister's son delivers the message to the commander, who secretly has him taken to Caesarea. The amazing part is how many soldiers they dispatch to transport Paul—200 soldiers, 70 horsemen, and 200 spearmen to take Paul about 60 miles! Paul was being used by the Holy Spirit (and protected by Him) in powerful ways.

Live the Word

What a story! Paul, a Pharisee, trained by Gamaliel, a persecutor of the Church, was now heading to the great city of Rome with 470 Roman troops to share His story! If we desire for God to use us, we must learn to daily surrender to Him and the Holy Spirit. It's not easy. Trading our plans and dreams for God's is not in our nature. We want control. What's interesting about giving God control is that He blesses our lives with more than we ever could have planned. Take out a journal and write your hopes and dreams for your future. Now, take that paper and put it into a fire, and give all those to God. Want a life that's used by God? Then you must die to yourself daily.

Day 4

Appealing to the Holy Spirit

Encounter the Word

Read Acts 24.

Explore the Word

Felix was the Roman governor of Judea and found himself overseeing the trial to decide Paul's fate. Meanwhile the group of 40 Jews who were trying to kill Paul had traveled to Caesarea to participate in the trial. Once again no fault is found in Paul, but the Jews were still furious and insistent that he was guilty. Felix was relieved when Paul appealed to Caesar, because it relieved him of the necessity of making this tough decision.

Live the Word

Making tough decisions is a difficult place to be in. It's a lonely place. Felix's situation with Paul is a reminder of how alone we can be without the Holy Spirit. Without Him there is no one to call for help who has true power to intervene. What decisions do you have in front of you? Are they about your future? I challenge you to call on the Holy Spirit! Write the top three decisions you'll face in the next 12 months.

Decision: _____

Decision: _____

Decision: _____

Take each one, and bring them audibly to the Holy Spirit.

Day 5

The Holy Spirit Creates Interest

Encounter the Word

Read Acts 25:1-22.

Explore the Word

This is drama at its best. There had been plots by the religious Jews to kill Paul, Roman political agendas, and riots. What else could happen? Paul now stood before Festus, who wanted to help out his Jewish friends—but again Paul appealed to the highest court of Caesar. Festus asked Agrippa about Paul's case. Agrippa was also intrigued by Paul and wanted to meet him.

Live the Word

What interests you? What keeps your attention? Is it styles, music, fame, fortune? When the Holy Spirit is active in a person's life, He captures people's attention. Think about it—there were plenty of other activities these top Roman officials could be talking about and spending their time on, yet they couldn't help themselves. The Holy Spirit had their attention, creating a captive audience of the world's most powerful people. What draws other people to you? Do you lean on what the world values, or do you allow the Holy Spirit to show through you? Do you have the integrity and passion that marked so many of the believers who have gone before you? You're special because God created you, but you're made attractive to others by the Holy Spirit's power in your life. If the things that make you interesting are things that your culture says are important, give those over to God. Ask the Holy Spirit to once again take control of your whole life today, and make you a living witness.

Entering In #12

Helper

Contemplation

There's one word that sends a message of urgency, a word that calls anyone and everyone to its sound. It comes with the understanding that time is essential and that all other options have been exhausted. That word is "help." You've used it to ask for assistance when you were stuck or perhaps to get you out of something you couldn't get out of yourself. We all need help at one time or another. God knew that all his children would need spiritual help—so he sent a "Helper," who is the Holy Spirit. This "Helper" actually led the way throughout the story of Acts. He captured Paul's heart, gave disciples courage, freed them from prison, used them to heal, and gave them wisdom and understanding.

Communication

The Holy Spirit answers our call for help before we even know to cry out for it. Read John 14 and answer the following questions:

- Who did Jesus ask His Father to send to us?
- In verse 12, what did Jesus say about how the Holy Spirit helps us?
- How often is He available?
- Who has the Holy Spirit within?

- What does the Holy Spirit teach you?

When you decided to receive Jesus' gift of salvation and placed Him as Lord of your life, you received a deposit on His promise. That deposit is something no person can steal. The Holy Spirit is your lifetime "Helper."

Community

In a way, the Holy Spirit helps us so that we can in turn be used by Him to help others. In other words, we can be very selfish Christians unless we begin to take our eyes off ourselves and let Him turn our eyes toward others. Jesus said that it's better to give than to receive. We need to start giving our lives away under the leading of the Spirit. This week look for opportunities to give. That isn't limited to material possessions like money and tangible gifts but also involves lasting gifts of our time, love, care, and prayer. Who have you given to lately? Who do you know who needs help? Who is shouting for help? In your small group, challenge each other to work together to help someone else.

Day 1

The Retelling

Encounter the Word

Read Acts 25:23—26:32.

Explore the Word

In today's text we find Paul standing before King Agrippa, delivering his defense of himself and his beliefs. Once again Paul uses the opportunity to tell his story—which is of course also the story of God at work in his life.

Let's quickly retell the story ourselves. Think of all that the Holy Spirit had done in and through Paul as he saturated himself in the Holy Spirit and followed His leadings—from his conversion in Acts 9 to being sent out in Acts 13; from his missionary trips, preaching and establishing communities of Christ followers, to his arrest and trials; all the letters he wrote, which we can still read today; all the people the Holy Spirit touched through him. It's truly amazing to consider it all.

Take a few minutes to reread Paul's defense before King Agrippa once more. What impacts you about what Paul was saying and how he said it? What kind of impact do you think Paul's words were having on King Agrippa and those listening? What do you think about the incredible drama of verses 24-29?

What I find amazing is when he retold his story this time, Paul left out so much—the pain, the hardship, and the trials we've read about. It's as if none of that was really important now. It might have been all-consuming at one point, but now—after the fact—it had taken on a different significance.

Someday God will retell your life story. The pain, the hardship, and the trials will all take on a different light. What seems insurmountable now will be a footnote in the larger story of the Holy Spirit in your life. God will retell your story *from His perspective*—one that finds a place and purpose for everything that happens in your life.

What an incredible day that will be!

Live the Word

If you're having a hard time seeing how God will retell your story, take a bold step today. Call someone who knows you well and has a sense of the wisdom of God. Ask this person about certain situations in your life, allowing the Holy Spirit to use him or her to share a godly perspective on the happenings of your life.

Listen carefully. Listen reflectively.

Day 2

You Tell the Story: Part 1

Encounter the Word

Read Acts 27:1-26.

Explore the Word

Over the past 26 chapters of the Book of Acts, you've heard us tell the story. We've served as your guides through the retelling of the movement of the Holy Spirit in the lives of His followers in the Early Church. We leave you to dive into the last two chapters of Acts and the life of Paul. What do you see? What do you sense the Holy Spirit is doing? Where is He leading? How are Paul and others responding to the Holy Spirit as they pursue Him?

For the next few days we've given you blank space and a few leading questions to help you retell the story and to see how your life fits into the story. Enjoy this part of your journey.

What's the Holy Spirit doing in Acts 27:1-26?

Live the Word

How does the truth of what you've discovered impact how you will live?

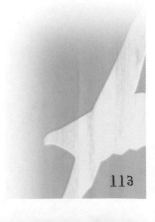

Day 3

You Tell the Story: Part 2

Encounter the Word
Read Acts 27:27—28:10.

Explore the Word
What's the Holy Spirit doing in Acts 27:27—28:10?

Live the Word
How does the truth of what you've discovered impact how you will live?

Day 4

You Tell the Story: Part 3

Encounter the Word
Read Acts 28:11-31.

Explore the Word
What's the Holy Spirit doing in Acts 28:11-31?

Why do you think the book ends as it does?

Live the Word
How does the truth of what you've discovered impact how you will live?

Day 5

The Holy Spirit in You

The same Holy Spirit who moved and inhabited the lives of Christ followers of the Early Church is the same one who moves and inhabits our lives today. He has not changed. He has not stopped leading and guiding His followers. Over the past 12 weeks or so, we've been on a journey—to see the "acts of the Holy Spirit" in the lives of the early followers of Jesus. Through the pages of the Scriptures we've seen Him transform lives and cities, heal people, and set people free.

What about today? What about us? What is the Holy Spirit doing in our midst? What does He want to do?

Take the rest of today reflecting on what you've learned and experienced over the past 12 weeks.

What have you learned about the Holy Spirit?

What impacted you about the early followers of Jesus?

What have you learned about yourself over the past 12 weeks through the Book of Acts?

How will what you've learned change the way you live?

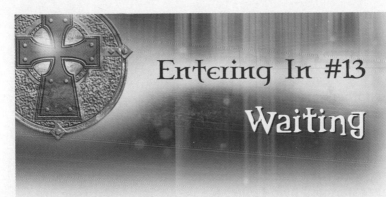

Entering In #13

Waiting

Contemplation

None of us really like to wait, do we?

It's the anticipation, the hoping, the unfulfilled desired end that drives us crazy when we wait. We live in a society of people who believe that we should have what we want when we want it and how we want it. We have microwave ovens, car pool lanes, and lunch menu items that are guaranteed to be ready in less than 15 minutes. We want it now.

We want closure, finality. We want everything to have an ending, nothing left open and hanging. We want resolution, a resting place, and an end to the story (preferably one that turns out how we want it).

Waiting means that we lack the final chapter.

Isn't it interesting that ending and resolution are not what we get in the Book of Acts? "Boldly and without hindrance he preached the kingdom of God and taught about the Lord Jesus Christ" (28:31) are the last words penned by Luke. No resolution. No ending. No sense of what happened to Paul next.

The beauty of the ending of the Book of Acts is this—it never truly ended. The Book of Acts is still being written today. It is being written in the heart and souls of people who, like the early Christ followers, are in a desperate search to be saturated and drenched in the Holy Spirit —to have their lives so in tune with the Holy Spirit that they are daily led and guided by Him.

You are a part of that story. Every day you live your life is another verse, another chapter being written in the greater story of the "Acts of the Holy Spirit." So when does the story end? Some day.

But until then, we end this part of our journey as we began, with the amazing reminder that we are the beloved, being pursued by a Lover. He is our Lover, and we are His betrothed. So the next time you celebrate communion, remember that as you drink of the cup, you're saying, "Yes, Jesus, I will be Your betrothed beloved. I give my life to You. I will wait for You to come back and take me to be with You."

Until then, we wait expectantly for Him, living every day in the pursuit of and response to the Holy Spirit.

Yes, LORD, walking in the way of your laws, we wait for you; your name and renown are the desire of our hearts" (Isaiah 26:8).

Communication

It's tough to be in a place of waiting. How are you waiting on God? How can you believe and trust in His faithfulness today? How does knowing that you are a part of next chapter of the Book of Acts impact you? How does it help you wait in holy expectation?

Community

At your last small group meeting using this book, take some time to share about the things you've learned during this journey with the Holy Spirit. What have you learned about God? What have you learned about yourself? How will your life be changed from this point forward?

Epilogue
The Face of the Fire

There's a legend that all firefighters know. It's called "the face of the fire." Firefighters believe that fire is a living thing, a sort of mystical entity. When a fire is captured in a photo, firefighters believe that they have the ability to capture an image of the "face" of the fire. Ask a firefighter—he or she knows. Look intently at a photograph of a fire, and you'll see it—a face in the fire.

It's not a coincidence, then, that the Holy Spirit is often portrayed in the Scriptures and in art as a flame. Fire has always been symbolic of God's presence. Remember the burning bush on Mount Sinai? Remember Moses' response? He was filled with curiosity. He was drawn to it. Yet when he realized who it was speaking through the flame, he was filled with fear and awe—it was none other than God himself.

Drawn close. Holy fear. Reverent awe.

There's a fire in the Book of Acts, an intriguing face that drew Christ followers closer. It wasn't Peter. It wasn't Paul. It wasn't the face of any human being.

Look intently into that fire again. It's all across the pages of the text. What do you see? Do you see a face there?

Who is the face of the fire?

It is the Spirit of the living God, the Holy Spirit.